# DISAPPEARING ACTS

*Kim Rosenstock*
*Susan Soon He Stanton*
*Michael Mitnick*

**BROADWAY PLAY PUBLISHING INC**
224 E 62nd St, NY, NY 10065
www.broadwayplaypub.com
info@broadwayplaypub.com

DISAPPEARING ACTS
© Copyright 2008 by Broadway Play Publishing Inc

First printing: March 2008
I S B N: 0-88145-382-X

Book design: Marie Donovan
Word processing: Microsoft Word
Typographic controls: Ventura Publisher
Typeface: Palatino
Printed and bound in the U S A

# CONTENTS

# INTRODUCTION
## James Bundy

Yale School of Drama takes pride in the talents of its students in every discipline of the theater, particularly when those talents are expressed through collaboration on new plays written by students such as those who are represented here. George Pierce Bakers historic playwriting workshop was the first course implemented at the School in 1925, and the production of new plays has been central to training in all programs ever since. While the mission of the School and of Yale Repertory Theater embraces historical perspective and canon-based work, there is no more important task ahead of our students than creating new theater in the 21st Century, and they know it.

We celebrate the voices of the writers you meet in this volume. With the support of their dedicated and generous mentor, Richard Nelson, they build on a legacy of playwriting at Yale: rewarding us in their vital individuality and demanding our utmost attention to the promise they offer the future of our art form.

# DISAPPEARING ACTS
## An Introduction

Forgive me if I make this introduction a bit personal.
This volume represents the third—and final—volume
I have introduced of one-act plays written by first-
year playwrights at the Yale School of Drama. In May,
I will be leaving my position as Chair of the Playwriting
Department. After three years, I have many rich
memories, though none greater than from a course
called Drama 7, which is my first-year playwriting
course. For a whole year, each week for three hours
the three first-year writers and I meet around a
table in my office to talk about playwriting, which
eventually means everything—life, politics, art, theory,
philosophy, music, strategy, frustration, pain, anger
and pleasure. I have learned a great deal in this course,
about myself, my work, how I work and think, my
weaknesses and strengths as a person, teacher and
artist; and I have been inspired and pushed by these
young writers, not just as a teacher, but as a playwright
as well.

I remember, before beginning to teach, my good friend,
the great lighting designer (and Yale teacher), Jennifer
Tipton telling me that after her first year of teaching,
she realized that she had better live up in her own work
to all the ideas and standards she heard herself trying
to convey to her students. As an artist, teaching young
artists, you can find yourself shaken up; you can start
to hear yourself say things you hadn't even known you

believed. Jennifer told me she found her work growing because of these discussions, and I would say the same is true of me. I am a better playwright today, because of these students, because of our talks in Drama 7. And for the past year that has meant because of three very fine young writers, Kim Rosenstock, Susan Stanton, and Michael Mitnick. I am very proud to introduce them to you today. They are all experienced young artists, who "bring to the table" a rich range of talents and experiences.

Kim Rosenstock has spent many years shepherding some of the finest young playwrights who have come through New York in the past decade—as a producer for such companies as Under the Radar, Ars Nova and The Underwood Theater. I don't think I've met a young produced playwright who doesn't know Kim; however, they don't know her as a playwright. Kim's play, LONE PILOTS OF ROOSEVELT FIELD, concerns a young female pilot, soon to be shipped off to Iraq, waiting alone on Valentine's Day in a Long Island mall that is full of history, both personal and national. Written with a light and graceful touch, this play hints at a much darker world, one just below the surface.

Susan Soon He Stanton was born and raised in Hawaii. Upon graduating from N Y U, Susan received the Sloan Foundation Screenwriting Prize ($100,000 of developmental support) for her screenplay about Rosalind Franklin, the female scientist who nearly discovered D N A's double-helix. It has taken her a few years to get back to playwriting; and it has been a joy to see her find again the unique pleasures of this form. Her play, THE ART OF PRESERVATION, is set on an island in Hawaii. Though a richly felt two-character piece, it also conveys and suggests a much larger canvas—one of an entire town, full of eccentric characters, deep conflicts, and exotic history. Reading this one-act makes one feel that perhaps this is only our introduction to a much larger story to be told.

Michael Mitnick came to Yale with a deep grounding in musical theater (music, lyrics and book), with four full-length musicals under his belt—all produced at his college, Harvard—and after assisting and being mentored by one of our finest theater composers, Stephen Flaherty. The play in this volume, LEARNING RUSSIAN, is a gorgeous and very funny piece about the pains of growing up, and all that is lost and overcome in the process. It is full of surprises and layers that slowly reveal their depths and perceptions, and conveyed in an ingenious structure and conflict. I won't say too much as I don't wish to give anything away, but know that this is a very mature work.

I tell my students that there are only two questions (or rules) that must be addressed in writing a play: 1) why did you write it? And 2) why should I watch it? If we answer these questions then everything—structure, style, form—will fall into place; and we won't be making those two great mistakes of playwriting: writing a play only for ourselves (a play needs an audience after all) or just writing to please others (we must also please ourselves). I am proud to present these three wonderful writers, each of whom, with these plays, has answered these questions honestly, deeply, truthfully, and with beauty, grace and humor. I will really miss this class.

Finally, I wish to thank Christopher (Kip) Gould, the publisher of Broadway Play Publishing, for his commitment these past three years to young writers and for his encouragement and support in the publishing of young writers' plays.

Enjoy.

Richard Nelson, N Y C, February, 2008

DISAPPEARING ACTS was first performed on
6 March 2008 at the Yale School of Drama, New Haven,
Connecticut (James Bundy, Dean) with the following
cast and creative contributors:

## LONE PILOTS OF ROOSEVELT FIELD

MISTY .................. Aubyn Dayton Philabaum
GREG ............................ Ryan Lockwood
RACHEL ............................ Brooke Parks
JACK ............................. Barret OBrien

MALL ANNOUNCEMENT VOICE recorded by Richard
Foreman

*Director* ......................... Christopher Mirto
*Stage Manager* ................ Kris Longley-Postema


## THE ART OF PRESERVATION

DESIREE ........................... Charise K Smith
DADO ......................... Christopher Grant

*Director* ............................. Jen Wineman
*Stage Manager* ......................... Iris OBrien


## LEARNING RUSSIAN

DANIEL ............................ Matt Biagini
MEG ............................. Aja-Naomi King
MAN ............................. Slate Holmgren

*Director* ................................. Jesse Jou
*Stage Manager* ...................... Jessica Barker

*For the entire festival:*
*Artistic Coordinator* . . . . . . . . . . . . . . . . . . . Brian Valencia
*Associate Managing Director* . . . . . . . . Stephanie Ybarra
*Senior Associate Managing Director* . . . . . . Jonathan Reed

# LONE PILOTS OF ROOSEVELT FIELD

*Kim Rosenstock*

# CHARACTERS & SETTING

MISTY, *female, twenty-five*
GREG, *male, twenty-five*
RACHEL, *female, early twenties*
JACK, *male, mid forties*

MALL ANNOUNCEMENT VOICE, *male*


*Time: February 14th, 2007*

*place: Roosevelt Field Mall, Long Island, New York*

# NOTES

MISTYs *clothing*: It is important that she be dressed in regular clothes—she should not be wearing a uniform.

*Music*: The songs specified in this play are meant to evoke the cheesy, guilty pleasure music that is played in shopping malls. If the rights for the songs listed in the script are not available then other songs can serve as substitutes as long as they are songs that one would not readily admit to enjoying and were released before 1995.

A constant soundtrack of music underneath the action is not necessary, but would help establish the mall environment.

*Slashes*: (/) in a line indicates where the following line begins to overlap with it.

*Elipses*: (...) do not indicate a long pause, but rather a brief trailing off in thought or inability to finish a sentence.

*(February 14th 2007. Roosevelt Field Mall, Long Island, NY)*

*(A projection of a shopping mall corridor)*

*(A large bench with a cushion. An unattended kiosk containing a collection of bear sculptures)*

*(An unseen wall detailing the history of Roosevelt Field)*

*(I'll Make Love To You by Boyz II Men plays over the mall's sound system.)*

*(MISTY, a twenty-five year-old woman, stands holding a pink, frilly bra in one hand and a braid of hair in the other. She holds these items throughout the play.)*

*(She speaks to us.)*

MISTY: I'm leaving in the morning to go over there. So it's my last night here, at home. Well, rather, here on Long Island outside of the Applebee's in the shopping mall which is ten minutes from the home that's not really my home because I haven't lived here for seven years and I don't even know who lives there now.

*(MISTY takes a deep breath and gestures to a sculpture on the kiosk.)*

MISTY: Can you see this? I know it's small. It's a sculpture of a family of bears. I used to want one of these sculptures so badly, but they're like expensive, just the baby bear alone is like fifty bucks.

*(MISTY picks up the sculptures and shows the audience.)*

MISTY: This is the mother bear, you can tell because she has pearls. And this is the brother bear, you can tell because of his blue sneakers. This is sister bear, she's got a pink bow by her ear. And this is the father bear, and you can tell he's the father because he has a beer in his hand. I remember the first time this kiosk appeared. I was in fifth grade, and my dad had taken me to the mall because I had just lost the school spelling bee. I was actually last place. I got out on the word "fuzzy", I thought the teacher said "fussy". They sounded similar. Anyway, my dad took me to the mall and bought me a bag of candy to cheer me up and we were walking around when we turned that corner over there and bam, there it was. The bear sculpture kiosk. Why bears? Why little bears dressed like people? The shoppers of Long Island can't seem to get enough of these little bears. Which says something about the shoppers and Long Island, though I'm not sure what, or if I want to know, and you're probably wondering why I don't just move if I have all of these issues with the bears. It's because I can't. I have to stand right here. I'm meeting someone here.

(MISTY *looks at her watch.*)

MISTY: Two minutes ago.  I'm meeting him here two minutes ago.

(MISTY *looks at her watch again.*)

MISTY: We agreed to meet here because this is his favorite part of the mall. And not because of the bear kiosk but because of that wall.

(MISTY *gestures to the unseen wall.*)

MISTY: It's called the Mall Wall. And yeah, it's a wall about the history of, that's right, the mall. So Roosevelt Field Mall is built on Roosevelt Field which is where Charles Lindbergh took off in his monoplane to make the first transatlantic flight in 1927. But the reason why the Mall Wall is so interesting is because it's dedicated to all of the men who attempted the flight from this very spot, on Roosevelt Field, and didn't make it. It's just so rare to see a big monument like this providing a chronology of failure. It's kind of spectacular. Lindbergh is nowhere to be found on this wall. Which is fine because you already have the Lindbergh Food Court and Lindbergh Boulevard's right outside, so, you know, we get it: Lindbergh's important. I always wonder if these other men...I wonder if they expected to be immortalized like this. I mean-they failed, you know? Most of them failed and *died failing.* But I wonder if they would have thought this was worth it, if this small amount of fame, this permanent record of their existence, was what they were after. Yes, it's a legacy of failure, of poor planning, of shoddy skill, but it's out here, for everyone to read about and see, which is more than most people can say.

(GREG *enters. He walks right past* MISTY *and she stares at him the whole way. He walks offstage and then he walks back onstage.*)

GREG: No way. No way. No fucking way. *Misty?*

MISTY: Oh, wow. Um...

GREG: It starts with a "G" and ends/ with a "reg".

MISTY: Greg. Wow, long time.

GREG: Holy shit. AAAhhhh!!!

(GREG *goes to hug* MISTY *and then turns it into some other gesture when it becomes clear she isn't the hugging type.*

MISTY: O K.

GREG: So what are you doing here? Oh, hey, dude, I heard you...that you were going...getting sent... I read about it in the paper. "One of Rosedale's own"...blah blah.

MISTY: Yeah, that's right. I'm shippin' out. Outta here like Vladamir.

GREG: What?

MISTY: Yeah, I'm leaving tomorrow./ Wait, it was in the paper?

GREG: So what's it like flying planes?

MISTY: It's great. I didn't know it was in the paper.

GREG: Yeah man, with a picture too. Shit. Misty. Misty Rollins. A pilot. In the Air Force.

MISTY: Marines. (*To us*) Greg is not the guy Im waiting for, by the way.

GREG: *Marines.* Well that's just fucking badass. Who ever would have guessed it? Dude, not me. I can't believe I ran into you, here, tonight. I mean, it's like fate, like I never come here, but it's Valentine's Day so there's a sale at Lacies & Pasties.

(MISTY *holds up her bra.*)

MISTY: Don't I know it.

GREG: Right...

MISTY: What? Does this bra make you uncomfortable?

GREG: No. What's in the other hand?

MISTY: My hair.

GREG: Cool, cool...Hey, remember in fourth grade when I tried to kiss you?

MISTY: Yep. That was like fifteen years ago.

GREG: So do you have a boyfriend?

MISTY: No, and I'm not really looking to meet someone right now. You know, the timing...

GREG: But it's V-Day. You know? Dude, make love not war. V-Day instead of D-Day. But seriously, hey, I'm really glad you bought that bra. I bought some caramel-flavored panties for Charlotte. (*He grins knowingly.*) You know what I mean?

MISTY: If you mean you bought her caramel panties, then yes.

GREG: So are you afraid to die?

MISTY: What?

GREG: I'm sorry, that was a stupid thing to ask. But hey, you look really good. Like really physically fit. Not butch or anything. Just really solid. Like, really—

MISTY: —So, who's Charlotte?

GREG: Oh, my wife. She's pregnant. Wait, are you not on my big e-mail list? I send out big life updates in December and June. It's gonna be our second kid. I've already got a two year-old, Hannah.

MISTY: Congratulations.

GREG: Yeah. Children. These panties are gonna be way too small for Charlotte's huge ass. I mean, when she's pregnant her ass just becomes like five times the size of the rest of her body. It's like I'm married to my wife and the elephant that's attached to her back. But hey, you aren't still living around here, are you?

MISTY: No. I live near base.

GREG: *Base. Awesome.*

MISTY: I'm only here for tonight. I fly back in the morning. And then I ship out tomorrow night.

GREG: So why are you at the mall? Last supper at Applebee's?

MISTY: Last Supper?

GREG: No, I didn't mean—the important part of that sentence was "Applebee's".

MISTY: I'm meeting someone here.

GREG: Oh, you've got a date? With who?

(GREG *gets a call on his cell phone.*)

GREG: Shit, hold that thought. (*He takes the call and walks off talking.*) Hi, what's up? Seriously? Again? How is that even *possible*? Ok, fine. I'll pick up some more Febreze... (*He exits.*)

MISTY: (*To us*) That's Greg. We went to school together for fourteen years. Haven't seen each other since high school. (*To herself*) Bye, Greg. (*She looks at her watch. Under her breath*) Shit... (*She looks at her watch.*) It's not that I need him to come here tonight. Really. This is more for him than for me. Me, I'm totally ok with just packing up and leaving in the middle of the night. You have to be ok with that. The other officers in my squadron, most of them are married, some have kids, and they've got to be ok with just leaving at four a.m. Saying goodbye to their families maybe forever. (*She looks at her watch.*) Just last month my friend Paul was being deployed and he told me how he was gonna spend his last night with his wife recreating their honeymoon in his condo. They had gone to Mexico, so Paul cooked her a whole Mexican feast and he learned how to play *Guantanamara* on the guitar and serenaded her. Then they went outside and swam in their pool, pretending it was The Pacific Ocean. And then they came inside the house and put their baby, whose name is Josephine, they put Josephine in between them in bed and Paul told her he wanted to fall asleep staring at his beautiful family. So he did that. And then four A M came. They had agreed they wouldn't cry. But they couldn't stop. She drove him to the base crying all the way. They parted and she watched him disappear into one of the buildings that looks like all of the other buildings.

But Paul's squadron didn't end up leaving that day. There were delays. They wouldn't be leaving until the next morning. So one of Paul's buddies drove him home. And Paul's wife was beside herself with joy when he returned. But then it happened again the next day. They said their goodbyes, and he left and sat around on the base for a while with his squadron and news came that they wouldn't be leaving for two *more* days. So he went back home. And then in two days the same thing happened again. And it went on like this for two weeks, until finally, she told him to stay on base, to stop coming home because she couldn't take it any more. So he listened. And he left one morning-without her knowing, without her crying, without her watching him go.

Anyway, it's better for me because I'm on my own, and goodbyes aren't a big part of my life. Which is good. I don't really want anyone who will cry when I leave or worse, try to get me to stay. Someone saying, "Don't go." I just couldn't deal with that. No, the only thing I need to deal with are my two fish. I need to flush them down the toilet. I figure at least it'll happen fast and they'll have each other as they get sucked down into the toilet bowl. They won't have to go it alone. It's kind of sweet. So, yeah, I thought that would be it. Pack. Flush the fish. Lock up. Ship off. But then he called me and said he wanted to say goodbye, in person, would I come home? So here I am.

(RACHEL *enters. She is in her early twenties, and dressed in a very tight-fitting, revealing, red dress. She is out of breath.*)

RACHEL: Misty! You're still here....ahhh I can't breath. They turned off the escalators. Had to...walk...

(RACHEL *bends over and puts up one finger indicating "wait." MISTY gets down on the same level and they begin to have their conversation upside down.*)

MISTY: You seem out of breath.

RACHEL: Oh, good observation, Sherlock. Where's Holmes? Better tell Holmes.

MISTY: Sherlock *is* Holmes. I think you mean...
Watson? / I'm pretty sure...

RACHEL: No, I meant Holmes. O K?

MISTY: O K. Hey, do you want to maybe try that bench
over there?

*(They both look towards the bench.)*

RACHEL: Yeah, let's go.

*(They go to the bench and sit down.)*

MISTY: So what's going on? I thought you had a...

RACHEL: A date? A chance at making a connection with
another human being? A reprieve from my "table for
one" status at restaurants, which sometimes translates
into the *counter? Just because I'm alone doesn't mean I
should have to sit on a swivel stool instead of a chair.*

MISTY: *(To us)* This is my little sister, Rachel. I arranged
to stay with her last night. And when I did that I
assumed she had a couch or a futon, or even a big chair
for me to sleep on, but it turns out, she just has her bed.
So, we shared it. But tonight being Valentine's Day and
all, well, let's just say I probably won't be able to share
the bed with her. Now some people might say she's
easy and desperate but that's not it, she's just... So I
agreed to find somewhere else to stay tonight. *(She looks
at her watch.)*

RACHEL: I mean, you know, dining alone and *dying
alone* are two very different things. And one doesn't
necessarily lead to the other. Are you even listening
to me, *Misty*? Earth to Misty... *(She claps loudly.)* Pay
attention to me, godammit, I'm having a crisis. *(She
looks to the heavens.)* Couldn't? Couldn't you have given
me a break on Valen-fucking-tine's Fucking Day??

MISTY: Um, are you talking to God? Because...I don't/
think that's...

RACHEL: There is no God!

*(A chime is heard over the mall's loudspeaker system.)*

MALL ANNOUNCEMENT VOICE: Attention, Roosevelt Field Shoppers, the mall will be closing in fifteen minutes. Please make your final purchases and make your way to the nearest exit. Happy Valentine's Day.

*(Chimes again followed by Whitney Houstons* And I Will Always Love You*)*

RACHEL: So he shows up at my door *early.* O K? He was early. I mean, *who's early to a blind date? That's just rude.*

*(RACHEL gives* MISTY *a look that says "You know what I'm talking about right?" And* MISTY *gives a look back to her that says, "Yes, yes I do." But then she looks back at the audience to say, "No, no I don't.")*

RACHEL: And then he asked if he could use my bathroom. But my bathroom was still in use. *By me.* Because I was still getting ready, because he was a full eight minutes early. You know?

MISTY: *(Trying to relate)* Yeah. I mean, what did he think it was, a *job interview*?

RACHEL: Yes! Ex-*actly!* So, I was like, "O K, *Bob,* the bathroom's right there. It's just a little messy. Sorry about that." And he said, "That's ok, I don't mind." And I was like, "Oh you don't mind? Oh, that's great. I am so relieved I could just die." And then I pretended to be dead for a moment and he did the Heimlich on me, it was all very confusing because—

MISTY: —So then what happened?

RACHEL: He used the bathroom. Number one. Thank god. And then he came out and looked around my apartment and said, "Wow, they don't make 'em like this anymore, do they?" And I said, "What are you an architect?" And he said, "Yes, I'm an architect." And

I said, "That's right, I remember, I read it in your profile." *(She goes on talking, but we no longer hear what she's saying. It's as though she's on mute.)*

*(MISTY steps out.)*

MISTY: *(To us)* She just has to get it out of her system, it doesn't actually matter if anyone's listening. And when she gets going like this she stares up at the ceiling anyway. Watch.

*(MISTY sits down next to RACHEL and gets up again. RACHEL just keeps talking and gesturing wildly with her hands while staring upwards.)*

*(MISTY crosses to the Mall Wall.)*

MISTY: So, of all the men on the Mall Wall, the one who has always fascinated me the most is this guy. Can you see him? Ok, wait, here...can you see?

*(The projection of the mall is replaced by a projection of René Fonck.)*

MISTY: "Who is this handsome man who bears a striking resemblance to Hitler?" That would be René Fonck, the first pilot to unsuccessfully attempt the transatlantic flight from Roosevelt Field in 1927 and his attempt went thusly: His plane took off somewhere near Macy's. His plane crashed somewhere near Pottery Barn. Three crew members were killed. While he was having a new plane built for attempt number two, Charles Lindbergh made the flight and was instantly an international superstar. *(She gestures to the wall.)* But here, we remember René Fonck. A man described as... *(She reads from the wall.)* "Distant", "arrogant", and "abrasive". There's a quote of his, here on the wall, this quote that I just love...it says, "I prefer to fly alone...when alone, I perform those little coups of audacity which amuse me." That's how it feels--this job, flying alone, living alone...within the extreme structure of it all, there's this incredible sense of freedom.

*(The picture of Fonck is replaced once more by the picture of the mall. MISTY goes back to RACHEL who is still talking.)*

RACHEL: So after dinner he said, "O K, I had a nice time. Call you sometime." And I said, "Why don't you call me right now and ask if you can come back to my place?" I thought that was a really cute line. Right, Misty? *Isn't it a cute line, Misty?*

MISTY: Yes.

RACHEL: Well, *Bob* didn't think so. He said, "I've got an early morning meeting. Rain check?"

MISTY: Oh no,/ he didn't...

RACHEL: Oh yes. He did.

MISTY: Well, thanks for coming here to find me.

RACHEL: Oh, yeah, well we were just downstairs at Friday's. I had a feeling you might still be up here.

MISTY: Yup. But he's only like fifteen minutes late, so—

RACHEL: I'll take fifteen minutes late over eight minutes early any day.

MISTY: We're very different, you and I.

RACHEL: I know, that's why you love me!

*(RACHEL punches MISTY in the arm, but it ends up hitting her in the face.)*

RACHEL: Oh shit!

MISTY: You just punched me in the face.

RACHEL: My hand slipped.

MISTY: He'll be here, I know he's going to come. He doesn't exactly have a shining track record.

RACHEL: He's actually got *the worst*—

MISTY: But *he* called *me*.

RACHEL: I just can't believe you came.

MISTY: What's that supposed to mean?

RACHEL: Nothing, its just—yknow, would you have come if *I* called you?

MISTY: Of course.

RACHEL: But I *have* called you. How many times did I call and ask you to come home? And you havent come back until now.

MISTY: Rachel, do we really—

RACHEL: I gave him your number, you know. Me. Youre welcome. Its the first time he asked for it in how long? Oh yeah: *seven years*. Real nice. Meanwhile, here I am and— When I saw that article it was/the first time I even—

MISTY: Rachel, its just not/the same thing

RACHEL: Oh no, I get it. You dont have time for me in your fancy, important life.

MISTY: Rachel, this is ridiculous, you think I look down on you for being a manicurist, when in fact—

RACHEL: I prefer manic-artist.

MISTY: Good to know.

RACHEL: I just can't bear to watch this. You finally come home and youre just sitting here, waiting for him. In the mall. *(She stops cold.)* Wait a minute. Turn around.

*(MISTY turns around. RACHEL gasps.)*

RACHEL: You cut your hair?

*(MISTY and RACHEL both look at the braid in MISTY's hand.)*

MISTY: Oh, ha. Yeah. Supercuts. I figured...

RACHEL: You figured...

MISTY: It seemed like it might get in the way. I'd have to buy more shampoo.

RACHEL: Shampoo is like the cheapest thing in the world.

MISTY: I just didn't want it anymore.

RACHEL: So why are you still holding it?

(MISTY *stares at the braid in her hand. She notices for the first time that she is clutching it fiercely.*)

MISTY: I don't know. When ancient warriors went off to battle they would cut off their hair and give it to their lovers to remember them by.

RACHEL: Well it's not like you have a lover. What? Is that offensive? I mean, you don't, right? And also I'm pretty sure that only happened in that movie Dad used to make us watch, the one with the dwarves.

MISTY: Well, anyway. It feels good. Like I made the right decision.

RACHEL: And what's with the bra?

MISTY: Oh, this old thing?

RACHEL: Seriously. That thing is pink and has flowers on it. It's not for you, is it?

MISTY: Yes. It's for me. Any more questions? Or perhaps you can enlist the expertise of everyone's favorite detectives, *Sherlock and Holmes?*

RACHEL: You know, you make it hard.

MISTY: I know, it's hard dealing with me. So why don't you go e-mail a stranger about it, ok?

RACHEL: I don't e-mail strangers, Misty.

MISTY: Yeah, you just sleep with them.

RACHEL: I was going to tell you that you could come back to my place tonight and stay with me, since...

MISTY: Since you're not sleeping with a stranger?

RACHEL: Ok, first of all, Bob is not a stranger, ok? And second, just because you're older doesn't give you the right to go away for like *years* and then come back and call me a ho—that's discourteous. *And finally*, that bra is *pink*, Misty. You're not *pink*.

MISTY: I'm sorry, was that supposed to make sense?

(RACHEL *gets a call on her phone and gives* MISTY *the hand.*)

RACHEL: Hello? Oh, *Bob. Hello, Bob. (She puts her hand over the phone and turns, giddily, to* MISTY.) It's Bob! How do I look?

MISTY: Red.

(RACHEL *goes back to her phone.*)

RACHEL: Uh huh. Huh. *Uh huh....ahahahahahahaha...sure... (She covers the mouthpiece and talks to* MISTY.) So it looks like Bob and I are gonna go back to my place. You'll be able to find a place to stay tonight. Right? I'll drive you back to the airport in the morning. We'll get bagels. Do you feel like I'm being a bad person? I just want to have sex. Although I'm sure Bob's going to fuck this up somehow—he's like some kind of smart idiot. So if you need a place to stay tonight just call me, ok?

MISTY: Sure.

(RACHEL *kisses* MISTY *on the head.*)

RACHEL: I can't believe you cut off your hair. *(She exits, talking to Bob on her phone on the way out.)* Ok, I'm all yours. *(She laughs.)* You're so *bad...uh huh, uh huh, hahaha...*

(MISTY *checks her watch. She crosses to the bear kiosk.*)

(*Mall announcement chimes.*)

MALL ANNOUNCEMENT VOICE: Attention Roosevelt
Field Shoppers, the mall will be closing in five minutes.
So if you haven't bought that special someone flowers,
candy, or jewelry this is your last chance. And for those
of you who don't have a special someone, don't
fret...love is in the air...

(*Tom Jones'* Love Is In The Air *comes on.*)

(MISTY *moves over to the Mall Wall and talks to the
audience.*)

MISTY: Now, the Mall Wall is really just the tip of the
iceberg. Way back in the early nineties when they
added this new wing onto the mall, a person—who
I can only assume was fired—decided to dedicate this
whole hallway to the history of Roosevelt Field. So
yeah, at first this part of the mall was real quiet. Later,
of course, they would add more stores and the bear
kiosk, but once upon a time, this hallway was deserted
except for us.

(*The music changes to* All Through The Night *by Cyndi
Lauper. Lights shift.*)

(JACK *enters. He is dressed in regular clothes, but on his head
he wears aviator goggles. He speaks with a fake French
accent.*)

JACK: Hi, Misty.

MISTY: Hi, *René.*

JACK: No, remember, I like to be called (*He spins around
like a disco king*) Fonck.

MISTY: (*To us*) His accent was always the best part.

JACK: I am Fonck. The second greatest World War I
Fighter Ace. I love flying the planes! Yes? Zooming
over everyone and saying, "Bye-bye you bastard losers!
You aren't good enough to lick the inside of my
goggles!" I have dedicated my life to flying and being

alone with the sky. The rest of the world is just clicking and clacking out little existences with their little friends and boyfriends and families and parakeets. While I soar!

MISTY: Teach me how to fly, Fonck.

JACK: I don't know. How dedicated are you, anyway? A skinny little thing like you. Let me feel your muscles.

(MISTY *makes a muscle.*)

JACK: Hey...*not bad.* How come we haven't seen you around the wall much, Misty? It is not easy for me to express my feelings. But if I were going to go out on a limb—I would tell you that I missed you.

MISTY: I've been studying for the spelling bee. Ask me any word.

JACK: Thermometer.

MISTY: T-h-e-r-m-a-t-e-r.

JACK: That is very wrong.

MISTY: I stink at spelling.

JACK: So what? There are lots of things that don't involve spelling at all. Like flying! And dancing! Dance for me, Misty, and I will dance *pour vous.*

(MISTY *starts to dance.* JACK *joins in.*)

JACK: Hey. I like the way you move.

MISTY: I like the way *you* move.

JACK: I practice a lot.

(*They come together to slow dance to the music.*)

MISTY: René? / I mean...Fonck?

JACK: (*Clicking his tongue*) Tsk, tsk...

MISTY: Will you say it?

JACK: Say what? I do not know what you are talking about, you silly little girl.

MISTY: Come on...say it!

JACK: Oh, do you mean my famous quote? The one on the wall?

MISTY: Yes!

JACK: Mmm...I don't remember it.

MISTY: Yes, you do! Come on! Say it!

JACK: Well, if you insist, but I get very nervous about performing under pressure. It is very scary for me. Oh, I can't do it. Well, O K. Here goes: "I prefer to fly alone...when alone I perform those little coups of audacity which amuse me." Like this! Look out! Hey!

(JACK *dips* MISTY *to the music, nearly bringing her to the ground. He slowly pulls her up to him. They face front, he has his arms around her. She looks out at us, but talks to him.*)

MISTY: This is fun.

JACK: Secret fun.

MISTY: I want to tell my mother.

JACK: You cannot tell your mother. This is not fun, little girl, this is serious secret business. We must figure out how to repair my legacy. I was a famous fighter ace but now I am a laughing stock. A failure.

MISTY: No, you're not a failure.

JACK: I crashed my plane. I killed my crew. I didn't even make it past the barn of pottery!

MISTY: Noo....Fonck. You're too hard on yourself.

JACK: Comfort me.

(MISTY *pats his head as if he were a dog.*)

MISTY: There, there...

JACK: I do not feel properly comforted. Put your hands on my cheeks.

(MISTY *does this.*)

JACK: Look into my eyes.

(MISTY *does this.*)

JACK: Tell me that you love me.

MISTY: You know I love you.

JACK: Give me a kiss.

(MISTY *kisses him on the cheek.*)

JACK: Ay...in France that is not how we do...you know better, Misty.

(MISTY *kisses* JACK *on both cheeks. He puts his arms around her.*)

(GREG *enters and* JACK *exits.*)

(MISTY *is left holding out her arms. The lights*

shift back and Love Is In The Air *resumes.*)

(GREG *clears his throat loudly, but* MISTY *doesn't hear it.*)

GREG: So yeah, I'm standing right here.

(MISTY *stops.* GREG *approaches.*)

GREG: Are you doing tai chi? I've actually always wanted to learn how to do that. And I've also always wanted to learn how to snap. I can't snap. (*He tries to snap and fails. He sighs.*) So, I just came from Macy's, and two guys are duking it out for the last bottle of Chanel Number Five. It's freaking *hilarious*. I don't think Charlotte wears perfume but if she wanted Chanel Number Five there's no way I'd fight some other dude for it. It would be nice if Charlotte wore perfume. Sometimes she smells like bologna and once she smelled like actual shit. That was this morning actually. I mean she changes diapers a lot, so it's bound to happen but I really hope she showered because we're probably going to have to have sex tonight. When you give a lady a caramel thong/ she usually wants to put it on and fuck you, right?

MISTY: It's a thong?

GREG: Oh yeah baby. We're going for the gold.

MISTY: Um... *(She looks out at the audience.)*

GREG: Wow, I'm really opening up to you. You're really easy to talk to. Why didn't we ever talk in high school? If I could do my whole life over again I would, in a heart beat. Hey, is your sister still kind of slutty? I always thought she liked me. But sluts like everyone, right? I mean *(He grins)* they *really* like everyone. You know what I mean?

MISTY: Wow.

GREG: I'm stoned by the way.

MISTY: Yeah?

GREG: I get my weed off this ninth grader who works at The Foot Locker. He's undercharging, rookie mistake. Ah...youth, you know? It's a beautiful thing.

MISTY: I thought you said you never come here.

*(GREG looks at his watch.)*

GREG: I don't, really. Hey, why are you still here? The mall's closed.

MISTY: I'm waiting for someone.

GREG: Dammit, this just *pisses me off*. What is wrong with the world? Why are men such dicks? Sometimes I'm embarrassed for my gender. I mean, come on, it's Valentine's Day. Have a heart, douchebag.

MISTY: Well, I haven't given up on him just yet.

GREG: Hey, are you looking for someone to spend the night with? Because my cousin, Ed, he's at home right now, he's like the nicest guy in the world. And he's lonely. You would love him. He's got a beard and an iPhone.

MISTY: Hey, what are you still doing here? I thought you were going home. You know, to your wife and daughter?

GREG: Well, *actually*, I had to buy some Febreze because my daughter pissed on my armchair. And then I realized that I forgot to get her a valentine from her old man, so I got her this gift, but I don't know... And then I bought the weed and then I ran into Mister Pierre. Aw, dude, have you heard about Mister Pierre?

MISTY: (*To us*) Mister Pierre. Tenth grade social studies. He was my homeroom teacher. He gave me the perfect attendance award.

GREG: He slept with one of his students, got fired, and now he just wanders around the mall, babbling to himself. Every time he sees me he asks me, "You got someone to love?" And every time I give him a different answer just to get a new reaction. Today I said, "No. I only love my dog." And he just looked me in the eyes and said, "Woof." He's a total freak. It's kind of sad. But hey, it could be worse.

MISTY: Really?

GREG: Well shit, I bet being in Iraq is worse than being a sad, crazy dude wandering around the mall.

MISTY: Oh *really?*

GREG: Look,/ I didn't mean it the way it sounded.

MISTY: No. You look, O K? I don't live here anymore. You're just a civilian. People salute me. When I drive on base, they salute me because they have to. I own a

condo. I'm a Lieutenant. And I'm only twenty-five.
I'm one of like *ten* pilots in the Marines who is even
trusted to fly the plane I fly. *O K?* Have you seen
*Top Gun?* I am tom Cruise. That's impressive. I'm
impressive. Be impressed.

GREG: I am. I am. Jeez. And now I'm also, like, scared
of you.

MISTY: I'm sorry. It's just been a strange night. Just
being here is like some kind of...I don't know. I've done
a lot of strange things. I cut my hair off. And I bought
this bra. It was on sale. It has a silk flower in the center.
I've always wanted one of these. And I figured, why
not? Why not just buy it? So I did.

GREG: I'm sorry for being such an asshole, I didn't
mean it to sound, the way it... But I think I know how
I can make it up to you. Give you a chance to wear that
bra. I'm gonna fix you up with my boy, Ed, tonight.
He has a Jacuzzi with jet streams. I'll call Ed. Just say
the word.

MISTY: Greg.

(GREG *dials.*)

GREG: Awesome.

MISTY: Wait, was the word "Greg?" Don't call...

GREG: *(into the phone)* Ed, whattup son!/ It's El Greg!

MISTY: Hang up! HANG UP!

GREG: *(into the phone)* O K, there's been a
misunderstanding. Check ya later, hombre.
*(He hangs up his phone.)* I'm sorry, you sounded
interested.

MISTY: No, I definitely didn't.

GREG: Well...

MISTY: Well...

GREG: Guess this is goodbye.

MISTY: Yep.

(MISTY *and* GREG *stand there awkwardly for a moment.*
MISTY *looks out at the audience as if to say "this is weird..."*
*She turns back to* GREG *and they stare at each other.*)

GREG: You're not leaving.

MISTY: Neither are you.

GREG: Are we having a staring contest?

MISTY: I don't know.

GREG: Can I show you something?

MISTY: Sure.

(GREG *reaches into his pocket and pulls out a plush toy heart.*
MISTY *takes it.*)

MISTY: It's a furry heart. Is this for your daughter?

GREG: It's totally gay, right? Actually that was the first
word Hannah ever said. "Gay." Charlotte said she was
coming out to us. But I was like, "Charlotte, dude,
babies don't come out." She's cute but she cries
whenever she sees me. Still, I'm gonna keep trying to
win her over. I got my friend at Kid's R Us pulling toys
for me for her birthday. Hannah only likes toys that are
fuzzy.

MISTY: (*To the audience*) Sounds a lot like fussy doesn't
it? (*She squeezes the heart.*) You know the mall really
well, don't you Greg? Like *really* well. Have you ever
just stayed here?

GREG: You mean, when the mall's closed?

MISTY: Yeah.

GREG: That's crazy. You can't do that.

MISTY: (*Defeated*) Oh.

GREG: I mean. If you *were* going to do it, this would be the place. Because Applebee's stays open later than the rest of the mall, so the guards just assume you're having dinner at the Bee's. And this bench right here is actually the most comfortable bench in the mall because someone paid the guy from Sleepy's fifty bucks to put a contoured mattress pad under the cushion. And when Applebee's closes all you have to do is just hide under the bench for like five minutes until they lock the doors up here. The night guard, Al, generally leaves this hallway to the Applebee's people, but the Applebee's people are like high school retards who don't give a fuck. So yeah, this is a good bench to sleep on...if you don't want to go home...I mean, I guess... yeeeaaah....

MISTY: Oh. I see.

(GREG *looks at his watch. He looks at the bench.*)

MISTY: Greg, do *you* want to—

GREG: What? No. I—

(*Mall announcement chimes*)

MALL ANNOUNCEMENT VOICE: Ladies and gentleman, the mall is now closed. Please make your way to the nearest exit. Here's one more tune for those of us who haven't been quite so lucky in love-there's still hope, just because the divorce papers are signed, doesn't mean it's over, Jeanine. (*Muttering away from the mic*) O K, O K, sorry. (*Pause*) Thank you for shopping Roosevelt Field.

(*Chimes. Willie Nelson's* Always On My Mind *comes on.*)

GREG: Hey, I'm gonna go. It's good seeing you again. It's nice when normal-looking people become hot. You know? It's like the opposite of what happens to the rest of us. Lets keep in touch? My e-mail address is greggreggreggreggg@hotmail.com. Thats four "Gregs" and the last ones got three "g"s. Yeah, I always thought Id have a cooler e-mail address.

(MISTY *hands the plush toy back to* GREG.)

MISTY: Don't forget your heart.

(GREG *takes the toy and exits.*)

(MISTY *sits down on the bench.*)

MISTY: *(To us)* This bench *is* surprisingly comfortable. My commander says dogs and soldiers are the two creatures that can sleep anywhere. I don't like to think of myself as a creature, but maybe he's right... *(She tries not to nod off, but she begins to give in to sleep.)*

(*After a few moments* JACK *enters. He is in his mid-forties. He's haggard looking, but perhaps he wears a wrinkled blazer or nice shoes to indicate that this is one of his "nicer" outfits.*)

(JACK *spots* MISTY *sleeping. He turns to leave.*)

(JACK *spots the bear kiosk. He selects a bear, and puts it down on the bench next to* MISTY. *She wakes up.*)

MISTY: Dad. *(To us)* I knew he'd come.

JACK: I. Got caught. In traffic.

MISTY: It's ok. Hi.

JACK: Hi.

(MISTY *gets up and is about to hug* JACK *when she realizes that this is a bad idea. They sit down on the bench.*)

JACK: So you're leaving tomorrow?

MISTY: Yes.

JACK: Are you scared?

(MISTY *doesn't answer but she slowly puts her head on his shoulder.*)

(JACK *puts his head on hers.*)

JACK: Hey, I got you something...

(JACK *gives* MISTY *the bear sculpture.*)

MISTY: Did you just steal this?

JACK: No.

MISTY: Dad, you can't steal these sculptures. They're precious collector's items.

JACK: I left some money on the counter.

MISTY: Where are you living? Who are you living with? What's your job? Do you have one?

(JACK *gets up and goes to look at the Mall Wall.*)

JACK: We haven't been here in a while...huh? This. This was our wall. You and me. Right?

MISTY: Hey, you think you could...

JACK: (*In a French accent*) Say my famous quote?

MISTY: Yeah...

JACK: (*In a French accent*) Oh, I can't Misty, I am afraid that it has been too long, I have forgotten the words and I don't have my special goggles. Well O K, I will try *pour vous*. "I prefer to fly alone...because...I...like it." (*He drops the accent.*) Sorry. (*He sits down next to her.*) Look at you.

MISTY: (*To us*) It's been seven years. He looks smaller. And a lot older. He still smells like cigars. And scotch. We still have the same nose. He's still not much of a talker.

JACK: So.

MISTY: I was surprised you called.

JACK: Saw your picture in the paper.

MISTY: Oh.

JACK: You fly that plane alone?

MISTY: Yeah.

JACK: You happy?

MISTY: Yeah.

JACK: You gotta home?

MISTY: I own a condo.

JACK: You gotta husband? A family?

MISTY: (To us) When I was little my mother would put me in my bedroom for a nap, only I wouldn't go to sleep. Instead I would climb onto my furniture. I would see how high I could climb up and then I'd jump down onto my bed. When I was done with the stunt I would look into the large mirror over my dresser and report on the events that had just occurred. I would say, "So what did it feel like to jump off the highest mountain and land perfectly safe in a huge snowdrift?" And I would answer, "It felt good, real good." "Were you scared you would die?" "Oh no, never, failure's not an option." One day I walked into my parents bedroom and I saw my dad talking into his mirror. Only he was saying.

JACK: (Facing out) Oh god, oh god, oh god...

MISTY: (To us) So I went up to him. (To JACK) Do you remember, Dad?

JACK: Yes.

MISTY: (To us) And we looked into the mirror together and his reflection spoke to my reflection. It became a new naptime ritual. Mom would put me down for a nap and go back to work, and Dad would come home. (To JACK) Remember when we would look into the mirror together?

JACK: Yes.

(JACK *gets up and gives* MISTY *his hand, she pulls herself up.* MISTY *stands in front looking out while* JACK *stands in back of her with his right arm crossing protectively in front of her chest, pulling her to him. They both face front as if looking into a mirror.*)

MISTY: (*To us*) He left home right after I turned thirteen. My mom kicked him out. But once I got a car I'd visit him on the weekends.

JACK: This was how we would stand, you and me. I'd look at you in the mirror and say: You're small now, but one day soon you'll be old enough to date and you'll be the prettiest girl in school. The boys will be knocking down the door. All wanting to take you out. They're gonna be crazy about you. But you remember that you're daddy's girl. And any boy who wants to take you out is gonna have to get by *me*. (*He flexes his arm muscle around her.*) You see that?

MISTY: Yes. (*She squeezes the muscle.*)

JACK: They're going to be scared. Because they'll know that I will kill any boy who hurts you. I will tear him apart with my bare hands. (*He grunts.*)

MISTY: Bear hands? Like a grizzly bear?

JACK: No bare hands. Like these!

(JACK *tickles* MISTY. *She laughs.*)

(*The mall shuts down and the lights get dimmer.*)

(All Through The Night *begins to play, but this time it's a different version of the song—perhaps just instrumental. It does not come from the mall speakers.*)

JACK: Do we need to go?

MISTY: No. We can stay. Let's stay here.

(*They stare at each other.*)

JACK: Misty. I was so young, I had no business being—
I didn't know what I was doing. I failed you. / I'm a
failure.

MISTY: Dad, no. *(She hands him the bra.)* This is for you.

JACK: Really?

MISTY: Sorry. I meant—here, I want you to have this.

*(MISTY hands JACK the braid.)*

JACK: I wrote you a letter once—didn't know where to
send it. I figured you wanted to get lost, that you didn't
want me to find you. But I came here tonight because
I wanted to tell you not to—I wanted to say

*(MISTY kisses JACK on both cheeks.)*

JACK: Dont die.

*(MISTY holds out her arms, and JACK meets her. They
dance.)*

## END OF PLAY

# THE ART
# OF
# PRESERVATION

*Susan Soon He Stanton*

# CHARACTERS & SETTING

DESIREE, *woman, twenty-seven*
DADO, *[Dah-do], man, twenty-seven*

*Place: a public library basement in a small neighbor island town in Hawai'i*

*Time: present day*

# GLOSSARY

*'aina*—land
*haole*—Caucasian person or foreigner
*kapuna*—elders
*uke*—abbreviation for ukulele, a small four-stringed
  guitar

# 1

(*A Hawaiian song plays. The song fades into the patter of rain, growing steadily more persistent.* DESIREE— *twenty-seven, sits at an old table in the basement of a small public library, surrounded by dusty boxes. She wears gloves and is thoroughly engrossed in the contents of a yellowed letter.*)

(DADO—*twenty-seven, enters quietly through the window with a bouquet of flowers. He examines his surroundings then spots* DESIREE *in the chair. He smiles widely, hides the flowers behind his back and slowly approaches. Just before he taps her on the shoulder, Desiree suddenly turns around and screams. He screams and drops the flowers.*)

DADO: Man alive! You scared me. You know, you two look kinda the same from the back—

DESIREE: Did you just break in here?

DADO: Course not. Window was unlocked—

DESIREE: Its never unlocked.

DADO: That Tammy's sweater?

DESIREE: It's cold down here, she lent it to me.

DADO: That was nice of her. She upstairs?

DESIREE: Library's closed.

DADO: This is *personal* business.

(DADO *scrambles to pick up the flowers. He looks at* DESIREE, *she folds her arms.*)

DESIREE: She expecting you?

DADO: Wanted to surprise her.

DESIREE: We open at nine.

DADO: Desiree...you treating me like one criminal.

DESIREE: You broke into a public building. I should call the police.

DADO: Oh please. Look, her car's out front. I'm gonna wait till she comes back.

DESIREE: I'll tell her you stopped by.

DADO: Gonna wait in my truck.

DESIREE: Hope you don't mind sleeping in your truck.

DADO: What?

DESIREE: She's not here.

DADO: But she left her car behind?

DESIREE: Can't expect a girl to stay home on a Saturday night, can you?

DADO: Kay...it's Kauai so there's only so many places she can go, right? Could swing by Duke's or—

DESIREE: You aren't seriously trying to crash her date?

DADO: So it is one date.

DESIREE: Dado...

DADO: If I don't talk to her tonight, I going burst.

DESIREE: Well, don't do it in here.

DADO: Ouch. You know, Im sensing plenty of friction over here.

DESIREE: No offence, it's just...you guys haven't been together in what...five years?

DADO: Don't gotta explain myself to you.

DESIREE: And I don't *gotta* tell you where Tammy is.

( DADO *starts to leave.*)

DESIREE: You won't find her, you know.

DADO: Saturday night, Desiree. Where are you?

DESIREE: Finishing my work.

DADO: And then? Seriously. What happens after you tuck in all your books for the night? Do you go home? Straight home? Is there anyone there to meet you? You get cats, don't you?

DESIREE: What does that prove?

DADO: Everything. Whole town knows why they hired Tammy. So no act like you hot shit.

DESIREE: I hired Tammy to take over the children's section. She's my friend, she needed a job.

DADO: No need get all self-righteous. You hired her cause you couldn't handle um.

DESIREE: The kids were outta control!

DADO: Tammy's got um under control.

DESIREE: She...does a good job.

DADO: So why's it different when she's around?

DESIREE: If you're trying to get me to say I'm bad with kids, fine. It's no secret.

DADO: Cause you think you better.

DESIREE: I think I'm better than a bunch of kids?

DADO: Better than just bout everybody in town.

DESIREE: Just better than you. That what you wanted to hear?

DADO: Sure.

DESIREE: Happy to oblige.

(DADO *exits.* DESIREE *returns to her work. He reenters.)*

DADO: Hey...uh—

DESIREE: No.

DADO: Tell me where she is and I'll go.

(DESIREE *returns to work.* DADO *fidgets.*)

DADO: It's raining hard out there. Been raining all week, only now, its getting real heavy.

DESIREE: (*Without looking up*) Persistent.

DADO: Yeah, real persistent. Like it's never going stop.

(DESIREE *does not respond.*)

DADO: Bet you think I tracked in mud. No ways. Was careful. Some of this stuff down here looks real old. Hate to get mud down here, you know?

DESIREE: What are you doing?

DADO: What?

DESIREE: You break in—

DADO: Technically—

DESIREE: To stalk my friend, harass me, and now you like talk about the weather?

DADO: If you can't think of anything nice to say...

(DESIREE *returns to her work.*)

DADO: 'Member Mrs. Oshiro trying for teach us the seasons? She'd turn red in the face trying for explain why the leaves fall off the trees, why snow falls in winter. Why'd we have to learn bout haole weather? Our workbooks always bout mainland stuff. Eh, you seen snow?

(DESIREE *pauses.*)

DESIREE: Once.

DADO: Lucky. I going put that on my list. Important stuffs to do before I croak. You know? I like take my boy someplace where there's so much snow, they don't know what for do with um. Maybe Lake Tahoe. Get skiing there, right? Then I can play poker too. Eh, you play?

DESIREE: No.

(DADO *looks over* DESIREE's *shoulder.*)

DADO: Whatchu you doing there?

(DESIREE *looks up from her work and gives* DADO *a look.*)

DADO: You like me leave? Or I could—

DESIREE: That'd be great.

DADO: Right. Kay. Have a nice night. Sure you don't wanna tell me where—

DESIREE: Bye.

(DADO *exits.* DESIREE *carefully picks up the same letter, she reads the letter to herself. He returns. He approaches her tentatively and clears his throat. She jumps.*)

DESIREE: Jesus!

DADO: Sorry.

DESIREE: I told you. You can't wait for her here.

DADO: It's pouring outside! Can't drive in that.

DESIREE: Sure you could manage.

DADO: If I crash and die...my blood going be on your hands.

DESIREE: Why don't you wait it out in your truck?

DADO: Roof's rusty. Leaks like hell. If you like, could sit in your car.

DESIREE: No.

DADO: Have a heart. For once.

(DESIREE *goes back to her work.*)

DADO: Desiree, please, it's been a shitty day. And I think I just reached an all-time low with you.

DESIREE: I don't believe you.

DADO: What?

DESIREE: Can't be raining that hard.

(DESIREE *stands up and goes outside. A moment.* DADO *looks around and sits at the desk. He puts on her glasses and imitates her. He picks up the letter and begins to read. She returns.*)

DADO: So you're right about that rain—

(DESIREE *sees* DADO *at the desk. He scrambles up.*)

DADO: What are you doing?

DADO: Nothing.

(DESIREE *puts on her gloves and delicately takes the letter out of* DADO's *hands.*)

DESIREE: What the hell you were you thinking? That letter's over a hundred years old. You were touching it with your hands? The oils from your fingers...are your hands dirty??? A finger print, right there—

DADO: Where? That's a smudge.

DESIREE: You smudged it. This might look like a big pile of dusty nothing to you but they're priceless.

DADO: Priceless, eh? So the library's rich? Tell um buy some new computers.

DESIREE: These are mine, or well...someone just gave them to me.

DADO: So you're rich!

DESIREE: Not...exactly. They were left to rot in an attic. Miracle they're in such good shape. I've been sorting them here. The air is dry...good for this kind of work.

DADO: So is it worth something or not?

DESIREE: Depends on who you ask. Letters, maps, the history of this town. Stuff no one remembers anymore. I'm the first person to read these things in over a hundred years. I'm donating it to the town when I'm done. I just...want to understand what's here. Be the first person to discover this lost history.

DADO: Wow.

DESIREE: So, it'd be nice if you didn't destroy it before I had a chance to go through it all.

DADO: Didn't smudge it, you know. That's...an old smudge. Ancient ketchup or something. Like me fix um?

DESIREE: No! I'd just like to get back to work. I can only do this when no one's is here.

DADO: Cause it's one secret?

DESIREE: A surprise, I hope.

DADO: I won't tell.

(DESIREE *returns to work.*)

DADO: Who's Lono?

DESIREE: You read that?

DADO: Why's he writing his wife bout leaving?

DESIREE: Are you making fun of me? Or do you actually care?

DADO: God, you really paranoid, yeah? I'm stuck here till the rain lets up. There's nothing else to do.

(DESIREE *gives* DADO *a look.*)

DADO: Desiree...I'm asking you cause I'm interested, kay?

DESIREE: A big flood wiped out most of the town—

DADO: When?

DESIREE: 1881.

DADO: Chee, nobody ever told me bout that.

DESIREE: No one talks about it anymore. Lono was the man who kept all the town's important papers. When he realized the town was gonna flood, he packed up all the papers and ran. Didn't even have time to go back for his family.

DADO: What? That's...really stupid.

DESIREE: He had to get these papers to safety. They were the only records. His house was destroyed but his family survived.

DADO: Doesn't make it okay.

DESIREE: He did what he had to do.

DADO: For some stupid paper?

DESIREE: When he got back, he was a disgrace. His family kicked him out. He left on a whaling ship. Asked his family to take care of the documents. Apparently, they did.

DADO: You get this stuff from Clarice?

DESIREE: Maybe.

DADO: Small world, eh? I'm related to this guy! Auntie Clarice always talking story bout what a smart guy her grandpa supposed to be. But you know...his family wouldn't kick him out. They wouldn't have to say a thing. It was shame that get him, from the whole community. Lost his priorities. Gotta take care of your family first. Your blood.

DESIREE: Risked his life for something greater than himself. He saved the history of the town.

DADO: What history? How can it matter when it's been sitting in the attic of my ninety-year-old auntie who steals croutons from salad bars?

DESIREE: This means something—

DADO: She shovels them into her purse—

DESIREE: I'm gonna make everyone understand.

DADO: You don't get it, Des. Your neighbors, your family's in danger...and first thing you do is...save a stack of paper? It's not right. It's not natural.

DESIREE: He understood the greater good. How to really help people.

DADO: You know why the ancient Hawaiians didn't have a written language? They put their trust in people. We wipe our ass with paper every day.

DESIREE: Paper protects the integrity of ideas.

DADO: Who's ideas?

DESIREE: Ever played a game of Telephone, Dado? You can't count of people, they get things all turned around.

DADO: Everything I ever need know was passed down to me by my father.

DESIREE: People die and nothing's left behind. That's why we write things down. So there's something left after we go. When I'm gone, these papers will still be here because of me. I'm giving knowledge back to the town. It's my legacy. Dado, what are you leaving behind?

(DADO *looks at* DESIREE.)

DADO: My son.

DESIREE: And what do you think people will remember you for? If anything.

DADO: You're like one of those fancy journalists who sees someone getting beat up but instead of helping um, you take one picture for the newspaper, pretend like you doing good. You don't know the first thing bout helping people. Gotta put people first.

DESIREE: How are we going to learn from our mistakes if we can't remember what they are? That flood? (*She holds up the letter.*) Your ancestor writes that it was caused by plantation owners trying to reroute the stream to water their crops.

DADO: So? Get the same thing now. The reservoir?

DESIREE: They didn't do it properly back then. It rained, a lot, and the water backed up till the dam burst. People died for someone else's mistake.

DADO: Chee, you're giving me chills.

DESIREE: Sounds familiar, doesn't it?

DADO: Should it?

DESIREE: Rich old man carving into the mountain. Same little town down below.

DADO: Judson thinks he owns this whole town. I don't have nothing to do with him.

DESIREE: Thought he hired you.

DADO: You behind your gossip, Desiree. Biggest job I coulda had all year was from Judson. Turned it down flat.

DESIREE: You did?

DADO: Told all of my friends, other contractors, not to take it. They didn't.

DESIREE: What for?

DADO: Some fancy fish pond for his new girlfriend.

(DESIREE *looks away.*)

DADO: HA! When he heard no one going work for him, crazy old bugger bought his own tractor. Let him build his own stupid pond if he like.

DESIREE: Don't you need a permit for all that stuff?

DADO: For Judson? Forget about it. (*Beat*) But when you talked bout those plantation owners, I stay worried, you know? Sometimes its more better to do one job yourself, even if you don't want to, just to make sure it gets done right, you know? (*He pounds the table.*) Man, I get angry. These rich old futs, buying up property, doing construction. Putting up No Trespassing signs all over the place.

DESIREE: The mountain belongs to the locals too!

DADO: Damn straight.

DESIREE: Take back the view!

DADO: YEAH!

DESIREE: Protect the *'aina*! Save the mountain!

(DADO *stops and turns to* DESIREE.)

DADO: Since when do you go up there?

DESIREE: Oh...you know. I like the option.

DADO: Oh man. 'Member camp? When the counselors found those books hidden in the bottom of your bag, dragged you out of the cabin and made you take up archery? You got so pissed. Man alive, I thought you were gonna to shoot Becky in the head with that arrow. Even back then you were so pasty. You totally hate nature, don't you?

DESIREE: Forgot what they found in your room?

DADO: Not books, that's for sure.

DESIREE: One of the other boys grabbed your pillow
and showed it to the girls—

DADO: Yeah, okay—

DESIREE: The pillow had a little, round hole in it.

DADO: Kay, I 'member, you can stop.

DESIREE: And everybody started teasing you, saying
you were humping your pillow—

DADO: THAT'S ENOUGH! Jesus, Desiree. I was more
embarrassed to explain the truth. We were poor, you
know? Everything had holes in it.

DESIREE: Lot of kids were poor.

DADO: Not like us. The tuna sandwiches? Don't pretend
you never noticed. Every day, one paper bag—just one
tuna sandwich, no lettuce, no mayonnaise, just watery
tuna. I was so shame.

DESIREE: I got teased about everything. Constantly.
Home lunch was the least of my problems.

(DADO *does not respond.*)

DESIREE: Camp. Camp was the worst. There was no
escape. They confiscated my books for Christ's sake.

(DADO *does not respond.*)

DESIREE: They made us hike. For hours! I hiked as fast
as I could, my legs were aching, I needed to be first,
I needed to get back to the cabin so I could be alone.
But you were in front and you wouldn't let me pass.
You kept getting in my way, teasing me. I couldn't
stand it, I needed to get out of there...so...

DADO: So you pushed me.

DESIREE: Didn't think you'd trip and go off the edge.
Thought I killed you—

DADO: Coulda killed me—

DESIREE: But you caught onto that branch. I pulled you up. You were fine.

DADO: Great story, Desiree.

DESIREE: Thought I hurt you. You wouldn't stop crying...

DADO: I never cry—

DESIREE: About your slipper that fell in the stream.

DADO: Couldn't afford new ones. Knew my dad was gonna be pissed.

DESIREE: I gave you one of mine. Fit perfectly.

DADO: Cause you had big feet.

DESIREE: Because we were small. You made me a slipper out of a ti leaf, didn't do any good, but. We hiked the rest of the way together.

DADO: Yeah...

DESIREE: Thought we were gonna be good friends, I just did.

DADO: Hardly saw you after junior high.

DESIREE: I...was studying in the library and you guys would peel out in your cars after third period. Where'd you go? I used to wonder.

DADO: You didn't know? Man, you were a loser in high school. We'd surf or when the surf was down, we'd park on the ridge. Drink. Some of the boys would play their ukes. If it'd rained and I had a girl, I'd take her sliding.

DESIREE: Sliding?

DADO: Ti leaf sliding? You never went?

(DESIREE *shakes her head.*)

DADO: What? What kine childhood you had?

DESIREE: (*Without sarcasm*) Tell me about it.

DADO: Yeah, seriously. I feel bad for you.

DESIREE: No, describe it.

DADO: Eh, it's stupid kid stuff.

DESIREE: I wanna picture it. Lono writes about doing it with his kids. Tell me about it...like I was really there.

DADO: Well...sure, I guess. So...um...yeah, we hike to the top.

DESIREE: Where?

DADO: The ridge, where the grass get slick from the rain. And...um...below there's a path of mud where people went sliding before. There's hale koa trees all around but ahead, it's clear.

DESIREE: Then what?

DADO: Kay...'magine you sitting on one big bunch of ti leaves. You holding the stems between your legs to keep you in place, act like one rudder. You control the speed, lean forward for go fast. Lean back for go slow. We push off. Pick up speed.

DESIREE: What do we see?

DADO: A blur of trees...guava and mountain apples.

DESIREE: More...

DADO: Um...the air. Air smells like wild ginger...fresh dirt. The birds are squawking at us like we just charged through their living room. At this speed, everything is liquid, streaming past us. Up ahead, the stream is at the bottom near the boulders. This is the dangerous part.

DESIREE: How do we stop?

DADO: Slow down.

DESIREE: How?

DADO: Lean back. You driving, woman!

DESIREE: Ha.

DADO: We crash-land at the bottom, covered in mud and follow the stream to the falls. We stand on the ledge while the water flows past, till our toes get wrinkly and white. Our bodies get hot from the sun, from the ride. We look at each other.

(DADO *and* DESIREE *look at each other.*)

DADO: Count to three. Jump off into the water below, icy cold, every time. One real ball shrinker.

DESIREE: This Pohaku Falls?

DADO: Course.

DESIREE: I wouldn't jump.

DADO: No?

DESIREE: That girl who visited, jumped off and broke her back.

DADO: No can worry bout that kine stuff.

DESIREE: I'd go swimming but I wouldn't jump from that ledge.

DADO: Tammy did.

DESIREE: Tammy?

DADO: She stood on the ledge with me, back in high school, her heavy, shiny Japanese hair flowed all the way down her back, god, I love that hair. She looked at me, I looked at her, and we jumped. In the water, her hair spread around her like it was one sea creature. I lifted her up on this cold rock ledge and...

(DESIREE *stops* DADO.)

DADO: Sorry. We made our son. Eight years ago, today. Best day of my life. I wanted to tell her that, remind her. Guess I'm sorta telling you instead.

DESIREE: Guess you are. It's a shame.

DADO: What? What do you mean?

DESIREE: You're a good guy, Dado. Better than most people realize.

DADO: The guy she's out with tonight...is he rich?

DESIREE: I don't know anything, just don't believe everything you hear.

DADO: It's not...

( DADO *realizes*. DESIREE *winces*.)

DESIREE: You weren't supposed to find out.

DADO: I drive thirty minutes out of my way just so I don't even shop at one of his god damn stores and she's *sleeping* with Judson?

DESIREE: We don't know that. She's seeing him.

DADO: He's an old man. An old horrible man with da kine...liver spots and pink eyes like one rabbit. He's wrinkly and shriveled up and...she's with him.

DESIREE: I'm sure it's not serious.

DADO: That fish pond. That Japanese fish pond he asked me to make. It's for her, isn't it? You knew. Everybody knew. This whole time I've been here you been laughing at me, waiting for her while she's out with him.

DESIREE: Hasn't been easy for her, single mom trying to raise a kid...

DADO: I know I haven't been the greatest. But...I've been taking finance classes at the community college and working more...and...I made one five year plan, one ten year plan... None of those plans work without her.

DESIREE: You have a kid, you guys will always be linked. By blood, right? Even if you're not together?

DADO: It's been years since she looked at me like I was a man. Like I get something to offer.

DESIREE: You have your plans.

DADO: Why didn't you tell me she was with him?

DESIREE: She asked me not to.

DADO: But even after I was waiting here, all this time.

DESIREE: I told you not to wait here.

DADO: That's the thing with you, isn't it? I actually manage to talk to you, like actually talk to you, then you do it again.

DESIREE: Do what?

DADO: Shit all over me with your superior attitude.

DESIREE: You weren't really talking to me. You were hanging around hoping Tammy'll come back.

DADO: Not anymore.

DESIREE: Good.

( DESIREE *begins to leave. He turns around.)*

DADO: Why'd you spend all that time studying anyway? We all thought you'd go away to some fancy mainland college and never come back.

DESIREE: That was the idea.

DADO: So what happened? Couldn't cut it, could you? Didn't even make it through the first year.

DESIREE: My mom got sick./ My dad told me to come back.

DADO: Yeah, yeah.

DESIREE: I didn't have a choice.

DADO: But after—

DESIREE: Thought it would be best to stay.
So I transferred.

DADO: Couldn't handle?

DESIREE: You never left.

DADO: I don't walk around like I'm better than
everyone else.

DESIREE: I could live anywhere in the world.
I get options.

DADO: You don't act that way.

DESIREE: What way?

DADO: Like you happy with what you got.

DESIREE: You don't know anything.

DADO: I know you. Known you for a long time.

DESIREE: You don't know me at all.

DADO: First day of school, your mom dropped you off,
called you Dezzy.

DESIREE: Oh please.

DADO: But even when we were kids, the name didn't
stick. Everybody called you Desiree right away.
Like they knew better than to call you one silly name.
(*Beat*) You even know my real name?

(DESIREE *hesitates.*)

DADO: See? Everybody still thinks I'm the class clown.
Not a man. They won't let me grow up.

DESIREE: Better to be called a clown than "that librarian
bitch." At least people like clowns.

DADO: But bitches are smart and sexy. Bitches are okay.

(DESIREE *laughs,* DADO *joins in.*)

DADO: Know how people are always talking about how librarians are really sexy and stuff?

DESIREE: That whole glasses, buttoned up blouse thing?

DADO: Yeah. Never thought of you that way.

DESIREE: Oh.

DADO: Cause I respected you...in your profession. But tonight, I sort of see that...repressed sexiness. It's in there, somewhere, I think.

DESIREE: Thanks...I guess. You know, I always wanted to be more like you in high school.

DADO: Stop lying.

DESIREE: My father told me, "brains don't mean nothing. Confidence is all that matters." He told me this because I'm shy and he wanted to punish me for it. I embarrassed him. You always had the answer...it was never the right one. You could talk your way out of anything. You knew who you were. I believed you could of been anything you wanted to be. Thought you'd leave town, hit it big.

DADO: Sure showed you. Des, I was a joke in high school. How could you think that—

DESIREE: After school I had to wait for the bus in the baking sun. You and your friends would cruise by in that damn busted-up convertible. You'd crack some jokes at me and drive off.

DADO: Always felt bad about that but didn't say nothing.

DESIREE: Doesn't matter now, but back then, I would've given anything to get in that car with you.

DADO: Well shit, I would have given you a ride in a second if I knew you wanted one.

DESIREE: Easy to say now.

(DADO *kisses* DESIREE. *It lasts for a moment then she pulls away.*)

DESIREE: You got the wrong idea.

DADO: Did I?

DESIREE: Five minutes ago you were crying about Tammy. I was just trying to cheer you up. Then you attacked me.

DADO: You wanted it.

DESIREE: Sure. That's what every guy thinks.

DADO: Was trying to loosen you up. You need it.

DESIREE: Where are you going?

DADO: Need air.

DESIREE: You can't drive in this rain. It's not safe.

DADO: Tell Tammy I came by.

(DADO *exits.* DESIREE *calls out to him from the doorway.*)

DESIREE: You forgot your stupid flowers! You're just gonna *sit* in that leaky truck in the parking lot? Fine! See what I care.

(*She throws the flowers outside and slams the door. She picks up the letter and sits down in a position as though she were sledding. She looks out over an imaginary slope. She chuckles to herself. She lies back. Sounds of rain*)

## Scene 2:
## Desiree's Dream

*(The sounds of rain are much louder. The opening strains of*
**Blue Hawaii** *by Elvis plays. There is a wail of air raid sirens*
*and a pounding on the door.* DESIREE *lies on the floor, asleep.*
*She wakes up with a start. She gets up and opens the door.*
DADO *enters. He is shirtless, with a large black trash bag tied*
*around his shoulders like a cape. He wears muddy boots and*
*carries an axe and a shovel. She stares at him. He resembles*
*an ancient Hawaiian warrior.)*

DESIREE: Dado, what in the world?

DADO: Dam gave way. All those big mansions full of
mud.

DESIREE: Tammy okay?

DADO: You the one I stay worried about. Why are you
still here?

DESIREE: Fell asleep.

DADO: In the library? Do this often?

DESIREE: Not...very often.

*(*DADO *produces another trash bag and ties it around*
DESIREE's *shoulders. He hands her a shovel, like a scepter.)*

DADO: Let's move.

DESIREE: Where?

DADO: Your house. Make sure your cats are okay.

DESIREE: I don't have any cats.

DADO: Seriously?

DESIREE: I know it's hard to believe but...

DADO: I brought you some boots. We gotta wade.

DESIREE: Pull around your truck. I'll load the boxes in the back.

DADO: Kuhio Street's waist-deep in mud. My truck nearly floated away. Everything's impassible. We gotta get to higher ground, quick.

DESIREE: We can't drive?

DADO: Not less you got a monster truck out back.

DESIREE: Took my bike.

DADO: So we're wading. Let's go.

DESIREE: No.

DADO: You gotta be kidding.

DESIREE: I can't go.

DADO: That mud's gonna slide down eventually, and that reservoir, honey, if that overflows, forget about it.

DESIREE: Dam already broke, what else could happen?

DADO: This is suicide. I'll carry you out of here if I have to.

DESIREE: Stay, just for a little while.

DADO: Why should I?

DESIREE: I could use your help, Dado. Strong man like you.

(DESIREE *cues* Blue Hawaii. *She sings to* DADO. *In time with the music, she pulls out a large plastic sheet. They unfold the sheet, each holding the ends, lifting it up and down so it billows in the air. He joins in and begins to sing with her as they stack the boxes on the table and cover them tightly with the plastic sheet. The song fades. They finish their task and survey their work.*)

DESIREE: Looks pretty water tight. We did a good job.

DADO: You aren't listening.

DESIREE: Water damage is devastating for books.

DADO: How about boulders? Mud makes the rocks slide...nobody expects a giant boulder until...BAM!

(DESIREE *jumps.*)

DADO: Pancake time. No act like you not scared. I see your goose pimples.

DESIREE: Course I'm scared.

DADO: You even know what you risking our lives for?

DESIREE: I've...seen enough.

DADO: What if only one little box was important, and the rest is just Auntie Clarice's coupon collection from 1957?

(DESIREE *hesitates.*)

DADO: I'm just saying. Now what?

DESIREE: Don't know. We wait?

(*Sound of rumbling, flowing water. They climb up on the table and sit on top of the plastic-wrapped boxes.*)

DADO: Not for long.

DESIREE: You don't have to stay.

DADO: You want me to?

(DESIREE *shifts so she sits back to back with* DADO. *She leans her head against his.*)

DESIREE: Your boy, he okay?

DADO: Visiting grandma on Oahu.

DESIREE: That's nice.

DADO: Yeah...worked out really well. (*He laughs to himself.*) What would happen to this place, if it floods?

DESIREE: The mud'll be so thick, you can't see the checkout line.

DADO: Not the checkout line! Since I put my life on the line for you, can you wipe out my late fees from overdue videos? Is high but can explain, yeah?

(DESIREE *closes her eyes.*)

DESIREE: The book cases will topple over and fall on the ground. The books will lie face down in heaps. The computers will be ruined, the microfiche, periodicals, those are givens. Mold will settle onto everything. The book covers will turn soft and fuzzy, as if dusted in snow. Except on the Encyclopedias, the spores will be bigger, the reference center will be in full bloom. The smell of putrid decay will be overwhelming. A big toad will sit under a battered card catalogue. Mushrooms will sprout from the carpet. Birds will use the pulp from the books to build nests. The library will return to nature and sink deep into the mud. A few books might be saved, if we work quick. But not much. There won't be much left.

DADO: You need to get real, Des. How you going stop the flood by staying? You can get up right now and walk away. Take what you can carry, that's it—

DESIREE: I can't leave. Everything Lono saved, it'd be like it never existed.

(DADO *looks at* DESIREE. *They sit a moment in silence.*)

DADO: Eh, can I hear the rest of Lono's letter? I didn't get to finish um. Or shoots, did we wrap it up already?

DESIREE: I don't know why, it felt safer for me to carry it. Do...you want to read it?

(DADO *takes the letter carefully and reads it out loud.*)

DADO: I was taught to follow *nana i ke kumu*, the belief that a community without knowledge of itself dies. The young are expected to go to their *kapuna* for answers. When I was a boy, the meaning felt didactic. "Be quiet

and listen to your elders." But I have come to realize
that the philosophy instructs us to go to the source
of life itself, to observe lessons in nature. *Kumu* is the
trunk of a tree, the base of a mountain. *Nana* is the
source of waves, a beginning, a creation. *Nana i ke kumu*,
the source of going. But going where, doing what?
I never found out. I met a man from New York. He asks
me if the Hawaiians have as many words for the sea as
the Eskimos do for snow. I teach him some phrases, he
repeats after me in a sing-song voice. With every word,
I am reminded of you.

(DESIREE *translates the Hawaiian for* DADO.)

DADO: *Ka po'ina nalu—*

DESIREE: The shore.

DADO: *Ke kai kohala—*

DESIREE: The shallow sea.

DADO: *Ke kai 'ele—*

DESIREE: The dark sea.

DADO: *Ke kua mauna—*

DESIREE: The mountain top.

DADO: *Ka wao akua—*

DESIREE: The land of the gods.

DADO: *Ka wao kanaka—*

DESIREE: The land of the people below.

DADO: *Kauhale—*

DESIREE: Home.

DADO: That Lono guy was one sad dude.

DESIREE: Now don't you see why he had to do it?

DADO: If he had to do it all over again, when the flood
hit, I bet he'd find his wife.

DESIREE: If you kept on reading, you'd understand.

DADO: No. (*Beat*) Okay, be honest. If you was one firefighter in one burning building and the only copy of the world's most important book was in one corner and me in the other, who'd you save, me or the book?

DESIREE: The only copy? What book?

DADO: This is like a hypothetical question? Choose one.

DESIREE: Honestly?

DADO: Sure, why not.

(DESIREE *considers*.)

DESIREE: I would save you.

DADO: That's really nice, Desiree, but not sure I believe you.

DESIREE: *Why'd you ask?*

(*Water and destruction sounds.* DADO *and* DESIREE *hold on to each other. He sighs and buries his head in her sweater.*)

DESIREEE: Smells good?

(DADO *sniffs the sweater and nuzzles deeper.*)

DESIREEE: Like Tammy, huh?

DADO: Not like Tammy.

DESIREE: What are we gonna do?

(DADO *examines the boxes.*)

DADO: We wrapped up these boxes so good and tight, we could use um to escape.

DESIREE: What?

DADO: Could surf these boxes like the Big Kahuna, ride um all the way to the shore. By then the sun'll come up and you can finally get one decent tan. Sound good?

DESIREE: I don't like getting sandy.

DADO: (*Disappointed*) Lame.

(DESIREE *jumps up on the boxes as if she's riding a surf board.*)

DESIREE: Okay, then...Plan B! We're still surfing but instead we ride the wave right down Kuhio Street, right through the center of town, past the movie theater and the noodle shop. I've got big Annette Funicello beach movie hair and a killer pink bikini.

DADO: *Righteous.*

DESIREE: We wave goodbye as we leave town. We pick up speed as we coast down the mountain, through the bamboo forest. I navigate deftly past boulders that fly at us in all directions. I grab a mountain apple as we whiz through the trees, the fruit is cold and hard.

(DESIREE *feeds* DADO *a piece of "apple".*)

DESIREEE: The board slows to a gentle stop, right where we want it to. The boxes are safe in their thick plastic, away from the flood, the town, and anything that can harm them. We balance on the edge of the falls, the water falls twenty feet below. Our bodies are hot from the sun, from the excitement of the ride. We are covered in mud. We are eager to celebrate our success, our survival. We look at each other.

(DADO *and* DESIREE *look at each other.*)

DADO: Hold hands.

(DADO *and* DESIREE *hold hands. He gently touches her face.*)

DESIREE: I like you. I always liked you.

DADO: I know.

DADO & DESIREEE: And jump.

(*Lights out. Deafening sounds of water, cracking, and destruction.*)

## Scene 3

(DESIREE *is asleep, alone in the library. There is a knocking on the door. She wakes up, disoriented and opens the door.* DADO *enters.*)

DADO: I've been knocking out there forever. Thought about going through the window, but I know how you feel about that.

(DESIREE *stares at* DADO.)

DADO: Were you asleep?

DESIREE: I think...yes.

DADO: In the library? Do this often?

DESIREE: Not very often.

(DADO *sees the boxes wrapped with plastic.*)

DADO: What's all this?

DESIREE: Afraid water would get in.

DADO: Chee, you are paranoid. Just stopped raining.

(DESIREE *listens. It has.*)

DESIREE: What are you doing here?

DADO: Wanted to apologize.

(DESIREE *looks blank.*)

DADO: For...*you know.*

DESIREE: I overreacted. I didn't really mind.

DADO: 'Preciate it if you don't tell Tammy bout the kiss.

DESIREE: Tammy...right

DADO: Gonna head out. Just...tell her I came by, kay?

DESIREE: Sure.

DADO: How much longer you going be down here?

DESIREE: I'm locking up.

(DADO *hesitates.*)

DADO: Walk you to your car.

DESIREE: Brought my bike.

DADO: Too muddy to bike. Want a ride?

(DESIREE *pauses.*)

DADO: Forget / about—

DESIREE: Sure.

DADO: Okay...

(DESIREE *looks at* DADO. *He looks away.*)

DADO: Cats must be starving by now.

DESIREE: Actually...I don't have any.

DADO: Huh.

DESIREE: Meet you outside.

DADO: Be in my truck.

(DADO *exits.* DESIREE *surveys the room. She takes off
Tammy's sweater, folds it carefully and sets it on the boxes.
She lets down her hair. She takes the letter out of the pocket.
She is about to take the letter with her, but changes her mind,
and sets it gently on the table. She turns off the lights and
exits.*)

## END OF PLAY

# LEARNING
# RUSSIAN

*Michael Mitnick*

# CHARACTERS & SETTING

DANIEL, *mid-twenties*
MEG, *mid-twenties*
MAN, *he is not old*


*Place & time:* DANIEL*'s kitchen. The present.*


*Dialogue Notes:*
*A backslash indicates an interruption.*
*Bracketed words indicate the continuation of the thought.*
*They should not be spoken.*

"I could tell you my adventures—beginning from this morning," said Alice a little timidly:
"But it's no use going back to yesterday, because I was a different person then."
**Lewis Carroll**, from *Alice's Adventures in Wonderland*


"Life is really about moving on."
**Oprah**, from who the hell knows

# Scene 1

(DANIEL *now has a cheap kitchen table with four mismatched chairs. On top of the table are two drawing tablets and some chewed, yellow pencils. At a foot of the table is a plate with a half-eaten slice of pizza. In a corner of his kitchen is a mid-sized cardboard box filled with* MEG's *things.*)

(DANIEL *stands to one side, holding a mug of coffee.* MEG *sits in the chair opposite him. The rear chair is occupied by* MAN *who wears a suit. His face is obscured by the comics section of the paper, which he reads.*)

(*Neither* DANIEL *nor* MEG *acknowledge* MAN.)

DANIEL: (*Shouting, to* MEG) You're such a fucking idiot! How could you not have seen me?! How?! I wasn't even driving in your blind spot! I was in the real fuckin turn lane doing what youre supposed to do in the turn lane. *Turn.* And then you turned from your *regular* lane, your regular person lane, and didn't even look, *you didn't even look* and you smashed up the side of my Subaru! It looks like someone stepped on a fuckin Sprite can. Here. Here's what this is about: you didn't look and now you're blaming me. Right? ...It's your fucking fault!! (*Short pause*)

MEG: And then what did he say?

DANIEL: She. She said that I accelerated while she was turning and my insurance will cover the dents.

MEG: Did you actually say all those things to her? You actually reamed out a school bus driver?

DANIEL: There were very few kids in the bus at the time.

MEG: Jesus, Daniel... Well, I guess you at least stood up for yourself.

*(Short pause)*

DANIEL: I meanwell I *thought* all those things. But I *looked really* angry. Like *this. (Demonstrates his "angry" face)*

MEG: Hmm. Did you accelerate while she was turning?

*(DANIEL doesn't respond.)*

MEG: Daniel?

DANIEL: Well she was trying to beat me to the turn and the light was the yellow arrow! The *yellow* arrow! That's a *very* small window! Tell me what was I supposed to do, let her into the lane and then wait *again* for the light to change?

MEG: Yes.

DANIEL: *(Genuinely occurs to him)* Oh.

MEG: *(Almost amused)* It was a school bus for Christ's sake... *(Short pause)* The car looks terrible.

DANIEL: It always looked terrible. This is practically an improvement.It's a piece of shit. That's what I get for buying a car with eighty-five-thousand miles on it. It has no get-up-and-go! If it did it could have beaten a fuckin school bus.

MEG: So your insurance is going to cover it?

DANIEL: Not entirely.

MEG: Because it was your third accident?

DANIEL: No. Because I don't have insurance.

*(Short pause)*

MEG: Wait. Why don't you have car insurance? That's ridiculous. And illegal \

DANIEL: I know \

MEG: You could have lost your license. What if a kid got hurt? Or she did? Or *you* did? You could go to jail...That's really dumb.

DANIEL: If I had known I was going to get into an accident I wouldn't have cancelled the insurance.

MEG: That's the point of insurance! That's really dumb \

DANIEL: You don't get to insult me anymore. You forfeited that.

*(Short pause)*

MEG: So what are you going to do?

DANIEL: The bus only had some paint damage. I apologized and paid her off.

MEG: With what?

DANIEL: I wrote her a check. While the kids watched.

MEG: She took it—you bribed her?

DANIEL: Yeah.

MEG: You bribed a school bus driver in front of a bus load of kids?

DANIEL: It wasn't completely full and yes.

MEG: Wow. O K. So is that check going to bounce?

DANIEL: It's not gonna bounce! I paid her a thousand out of the one-hundred-and-fifty thousand.

MEG: Not this again \

DANIEL: You still don't believe me? That's great \

MEG: Well I'm sorry but the whole thing is a little hard to believe \

DANIEL: (*Slowly.*) One-hundred-and-fifty-six-thousand, four-hundred and eighteen dollars and thirty-three cents.

MEG: Deposited in your bank \ [account.]

DANIEL: Deposited in my bank account.

MEG: Doesn't it raise a red flag in the bank's system when someone deposits that much money into an account that has never had more than four-hundred bucks in it at a time?

DANIEL: Apparently not. I asked that.

MEG: And what'd they say?

DANIEL: Apparently not. (*Sits. Places mug down*) I'm loaded.

MEG: So are you going to show me a statement?

DANIEL: Um...no.

MEG: Why not?

DANIEL: I don't have to prove anything to you. You should trust me, simple as that. A great thing happened to me, Meg. An amazing stroke of luck. Finally. So you have to accept that.

MEG: Right. I have to accept \ [that.]

DANIEL: And, hey, what reason would I have to make this up anyway? What motive?

MEG: I dunno.

DANIEL: Maybe I'm trying to impress you with all this money and then you'll come back. Maybe that's it.

MEG: Since when do you drink coffee?

(DANIEL *shrugs. Uncomfortable pause. Looks to the box*)

MEG: Is that all of it?

DANIEL: All the stuff I didn't break—how's the shrink?

MEG: Physical therapist. Not mental.

DANIEL: I know. How is he?

MEG: He's good, Daniel.

DANIEL: Good. Um... So why do you think I have all this money? I figure it's from when I left my wallet at Baskin-Robins.

MEG: You think the person who found your wallet is trying to...hide money in your account?

DANIEL: Maybe. I had them change my PIN and give me new account numbers, so it doesn't matter what happened. Anything that's in my account stays in my account.

MEG: And it's just yours?

DANIEL: *(Smiling)* Apparently.

MEG: You can't spend it.

DANIEL: Like hell I'm not spending it. I can pay my \ *(Juts out tongue, brings hand to mouth)* I can pay \ *(Gags. Wipes tongue with hand, searching for invisible hair.)* Beh!

MEG: What are you \

DANIEL: I have a hair on my. Eh! Eh! *(Short pause)* Did I get it? *(Checks, moves mouth around a few times until satisfied. Long pause)* I don't remember what we were talking about.

MEG: You're going to spend the money that isn't yours.

DANIEL: I can pay my fucking bills! Things I couldn't afford. College loans! Car Insurance! Laundry detergent! Everything! I'm gonna quit my job and focus on drawing.

MEG: That's not a good idea.

DANIEL: You don't think I'm good. Is that what you're \ [saying?]

MEG: No, that's not what I'm saying. I'm *saying* that you just shouldn't quit your job...

DANIEL: *(Eyes her. Flips open one of the notepads)* The eye of the giant squid is as large as a basketball.

MEG: See, I didn't know that.

*(DANIEL turns page, reads off back.)*

DANIEL: Swans are the only birds with penises.

MEG: They can't put that under a juice cap.

DANIEL: It'll fit if I change "penises" to "dicks". I counted the letters.

MEG: Stop.

DANIEL: I get four dollars for each piece of trivia. So they won't use it, but I'll get paid. Four bones. Hell, I think it's plain fascinating. Swans with penises. That's great. Who wouldn't want to know that? *(Closes notepad)* The point is I don't need to do this anymore. I can focus on my cartoons. Someone wants me to focus on my cartoons. Why am I even arguing this? You can't enjoy things. That's your problem.

MEG: Yeah, that's my problem. *(Short pause)*

DANIEL: Finally I can focus on bigger things—like this. Hey, tell me if this is funny. I've been working on it for a month. *(Flips through the tablet, searching)* I'm thinking of sending it to *The New Yorker*. *(Sets down the tablet, picks up the other one. Continues search)* Uhh...here!

*(DANIEL locates it, flips cover over and hands the tablet to MEG. He smiles, waiting, hoping.)*

MEG: This is good. I'm impressed.

DANIEL: You get it?

MEG: Yeah. I like it. It's funny.

DANIEL: Can you explain it back to me, just so I'm sure it reads. Their standards are, like \

MEG: I thought it's not good to explain jokes.

DANIEL: Well, just describe it to me. I want to make sure. I'm worried it doesn't read \ [just]

MEG: I think you've done a good job; it's pretty clear. The rooster is telling the farmer \ [to]

DANIEL: *(Taken aback)* What? *(Suddenly hurt and confused. He snatches the tablet back.)* No, that's not a rooster. That's a building.

MEG: No, no. *(She stands and moves behind him. Points)* There. That's the rooster.

DANIEL: No, that's a building.

MEG: *(Tips her head to the side)* Oh. *(Short pause. Points)* Well then what's that?

DANIEL: Another building.

MEG: So where is the rooster \ [?]

DANIEL: There is no rooster in this comic!

MEG: Huh. *(Short pause)* I liked it as a rooster. Maybe you could \ [change it to]

*(DANIEL tosses the notebook to the table.)*

DANIEL: Forget it. I hate it anyway. I should have stopped working on it a month ago. *(Pause)* How is Doctor Harris?

MEG: I already answered you, Daniel. He's good. *(She stands. Moves to the cardboard box. Picks it up, takes it back to the table. Sits with box on lap. She is ready to go.)*

DANIEL: Work is going well for him? Steady? Good number of clients?

MEG: Yes.

DANIEL: I guess that's not a good thing, for the clients at least. They're people that are really fucked up, right? Accidents? Broken spines? Shattered...pelvi? He's helping them?

MEG: Yes.

DANIEL: I remembered his name. Doctor Harris.

MEG: I know you did. *(Starts to exit)*

DANIEL: I like him.

MEG: You've never met him.

DANIEL: Wait. Is he funny? *(She stops.)*

MEG: Yes.

*(Short pause)*

DANIEL: Is he as funny as I am?

MEG: You have different senses of humor.

DANIEL: Well, do you laugh more when you are with him or when you were with me?

*(Short pause)*

MEG: That's my mug.

*(DANIEL stares at MEG. After a moment, he spills the remaining contents of the mug onto the floor and hands it to her. Blackout)*

## Scene 2

*(Three weeks later. Hard rain. MAN still sits in his chair, reading the comics. DANIEL is offstage R. Sounds of a televised hockey game blare so loudly that it is almost uncomfortable to hear. After some time, MEG enters from the outside, wearing a rain coat on top of a dress, rain boots and she carries an umbrella. She hooks the umbrella onto the L chair. The pizza is gone. The plate remains.)*

MEG: Daniel?

DANIEL: *(Off)* Sonofabitch!

MEG: *(Removes raincoat)* Daniel! Would you please come in here!? *(Sits down and starts to remove the boots. It's a struggle.)* Ugh. Daniel!?

*(More struggling, MEG finally removes boots. After more time, DANIEL enters from right, disheveled, barefooted and in boxers. He is chewing gum.)*

DANIEL: Whoa. Where'd you come from?

MEG: Originally?

DANIEL: Cute. You always were the funny one, don't let anyone tell you differently. How did you get into my house?

*(MEG holds up her keychain.)*

DANIEL: You should give that back. Is it raining?

*(Short pause. MEG glares at DANIEL.)*

DANIEL: What's up?

MEG: You look awful.

DANIEL: You came here to tell me that?

MEG: No. Have you showered since I last saw you?

DANIEL: No. What's up?

MEG: You smell like a fish tank. I got a phone call from your mother...

(DANIEL *wanders back off to the T V.*)

MEG: Where are you...Daniel? (*Short pause*) Daniel?

DANIEL: (*Off*) Skate you Canadian fuck! Skate! What the hell are you— Woo Woo! Yeah!

(DANIEL *claps in celebration.* MEG *walks off R to retrieve him. After a few seconds pass, the sound is muted, then they both quickly reenter, she leads, holding his remote.*)

MEG: Where did you get that?

DANIEL: The store. Give it.

MEG: Right. How did you *pay* for that?

DANIEL: My money. Give it back, they stopped putting buttons on the T Vs. Those Panasonic pricks. They do it so if you lose the remote you're screwed and you have to buy another one.

MEG: How big is that thing?

DANIEL: Sixty inches. Flat Hi-Def L C D. 1080p. It's like looking through a window at an infinite carousel of mind-numbing entertainment. I can go hours without having to think a single thought. I love it.

MEG: How much was it?

DANIEL: Why, you want one?

MEG: Where did you get the money? You didn't put this on your credit card, did you?

DANIEL: (*More frustrated*) I blew the salesman yes I put it on my credit card. What does it matter? I can pay for it.

MEG: This is ridiculous. What are you doing? Are you going through something?

DANIEL: I just bought a T V with my money. How is this a problem for you?

MEG: Daniel. You have no money.

DANIEL: So you're calling me a liar?

MEG: I'm not calling you a liar.

DANIEL: Maybe I stole it? Holy shit—did that cross your mind? Maybe I stole the T V.

MEG: I don't know.

DANIEL: Oh my God—did it? Did that ever cross your mind? You think that's something I would do?

MEG: I don't know.

*(Long pause. DANIEL grabs the remote and goes off R. The T V sound returns.)*

MEG: Daniel! *(Short pause)* This is...[ridiculous. Would you just stay in]

*(MEG goes off. MAN is left alone on stage. A few moments pass.)*

DANIEL: *(Off)* Give it back!

*(The T V sound is turned off.)*

MEG: *(Off)* Holy crap! Where did you get this?

DANIEL: *(Off)* Don't touch that! Give it back!

MEG: *(Off)* Holy crap!

DANIEL: *(Off)* Don't touch it! Seriously. Put it down!

*(MEG storms back on stage. She has a pile of paper money. DANIEL follows her on.)*

DANIEL: That's not yours.

MEG: *(Looks through the bills)* These are hundreds. Where did you—why do you have all this cash?

DANIEL: It's safer in cash than in the bank.

*(Short pause)*

MEG: So no one can take it back. You did this so no one can \ [take it back.]

DANIEL: It's my money!

MEG: So this is real?

DANIEL: What did you think?

MEG: *(Sits down on* MAN's *lap. Picks up a boot. Begins to put it on)* What did I think, what did I think? Honest to God, I don't know what to think anymore...anymore...

MAN: Daniel.

MEG: Daniel. Whoa. I totally blanked out.

DANIEL: On my name.

MEG: *(She stands and paces, holding boot.)* Someone doesn't steal your wallet and then deposit money in your bank account. Don't you see how that doesn't make sense?

DANIEL: Maybe the thief is just monumentally stupid.

MEG: Or confused about how being a criminal works.

DANIEL: Why are you here?

MEG: Your mother called me.

DANIEL: Why would she call you?

MEG: Because she couldn't call *you*. She said you weren't answering the phone.

DANIEL: I've been really busy.

MEG: Yeah, busy. Then I called and you didn't pick up either. So I came over.

DANIEL: You were worried about me, huh?

MEG: Yes, *Daniel*. I was worried about you. (*Sits in empty chair. Puts back on boots*)

DANIEL: Did you tell Doctor Harris where you were going?

MEG: Yes I told him.

DANIEL: And what did he say?

MEG: He said, "I hope he's alright. Let me know if I can help."

DANIEL: Fucking asshole.

MEG: Are you alright?

DANIEL: Never been better.

MEG: Yeah, slamming into school buses, never been better.

DANIEL: I have money! That's what's been holding me back. I can finally focus on real work. I can... Do you know how awful it is to be embarrassed of yourself?

MEG: Daniel \

DANIEL: I used to have this trust. That I was headed somewhere. That I wouldn't be this...failure.

MEG: You're so young!

DANIEL: Doesn't matter. Everyone I graduated with is somewhere. Hedge fund, law firm. Someone changed the rulebook and it's different now. If you don't make it by the time you're twenty-eight you might as well kill yourself.

MEG: You're being ridiculous \

DANIEL: I'm not. I'm really not. Some people go to Med school; I got a PhD in Failure. I was blowing through my savings and google-ing trivia for four dollars a pop.

That was it. I was no where. *(Short pause)* Till one morning I woke up and I scratched my stomach and I put my feet on the floor and I had a thousand ideas in my head. It's so weird. I have a great idea for a kids' book and for a tear-off calendar \ [where on every day...]

MEG: When is the last time you actually slept?

DANIEL: Wednesday.

MEG: Something is different.

DANIEL: I usually wear pants.

MEG: No and no you didn't. Something else.

DANIEL: *(Looks himself over)* What?

MEG: I've never seen you chew gum before.

DANIEL: It helps me stay awake.

MEG: How \ [does it]

DANIEL: It's nicotine gum.

MEG: You don't smoke.

DANIEL: I know. *(Short pause)* Why are you so dressed up?

MEG: *(Self-conscious)* What? I'm not dressed up. *(Starts to put raincoat back on)*

DANIEL: You wore that any time we went into the city.

MEG: No I didn't \ [I wore lots of]

DANIEL: Uh-uh. I remember. You wore this. Did you get dressed up to come over here?

MEG: Spit out that gum. It's disgusting.

DANIEL: Uh-uh. I'm addicted.

MEG: To nicotine gum?

DANIEL: Those bastards will get you one way or another. Do you think this will kill me like cigarettes?

MEG: I'm not sure. It doesn't have tar or fiberglass in it, right? I'm not sure. I guess anything that you're dependant on, like caffeine \ [can't be completely good for you.]

DANIEL: Will you have dinner with me tonight?

MEG: What?

DANIEL: I want you to have dinner with me tonight. I've barely left the house in, I don't know how many days. I need to get out, I need to get out—I want to go out somewhere. *(Short pause)* I'm paying. I'm rich now. *(Short pause)* Or we could order in and watch the new T V. *(Takes out his cellphone)* You like...um...um... *(Snaps fingers, trying to remember...)*

MAN: Happy \ [Garden.]

DANIEL: Happy Garden. *(Opens phone)* I'm pretty sure I have the number in here...

MEG: I can't.

DANIEL: What? *(Closes phone)* Do you have plans \ [with Doctor Harris?]

MEG: I'm having dinner with Gordy.

DANIEL: Where?

MEG: *(Reluctant)* Franco's.

DANIEL: That's why you're dressed up. You know it's a shitty restaurant.

MAN: Daniel. Forget about it.

DANIEL: *(Quickly, defensive)* Just because they price everything six dollars more than other places doesn't mean that the food is any better. I've been to good expensive places. Franco's just sucks.

MEG: Daniel...

DANIEL: They put less stuff on your plate and you think that makes it gourmet? It doesn't. It just makes you *hungry*. I got a salad there once that was only a piece of cabbage with dressing spooned out along the stem. That's it. One piece of cabbage. On a fancy triangular plate. Guess how much it cost?

(MEG *picks up her umbrella to leave.*)

MEG: I just wanted to make sure you were O K \ [and to]

DANIEL: Bullshit and don't change the subject. Guess how much the salad cost?

MEG: I should \

DANIEL: How much did the salad cost?

(*Short pause*)

MEG: I dunno. Twenty dollars.

(*Short pause*)

DANIEL: It cost twelve dollars, but that's still— Dammit Meg. Why'd you have to guess—what—twenty dollars? For a side salad?

MEG: Sorry.

DANIEL: A normal person would guess seven dollars. Maybe eight. It's one leaf of fucking cabbage!

MEG: I'm sure it wasn't \ [cabbage.]

DANIEL: It was cabbage! (*Short pause*) I know my vegetables!!

(*A car honks twice*)

MEG: That's him. Thanks.

DANIEL: For what?

MEG: *(Considers for a moment then laughs)* I have no idea. It was automatic.

DANIEL: You didn't drive yourself?

MEG: He dropped me while he picked up a prescription.

DANIEL: Oh shit. Is he fucked up? Does he have chronic...um...does he wet himself or \ [something?]

MEG: The prescription is for me.

DANIEL: Are you \ [O K?]

MEG: It's my birth control.

*(Short pause)*

DANIEL: Right.

*(MEG starts to exit.)*

DANIEL: Hey. *(She turns.)* When I asked you to go to dinner I meant as friends.

MEG: I know that.

DANIEL: I just wanted to be clear about that.

MEG: O K. *(Long pause. She doesn't leave.)*

MAN: *(Putting down paper. To DANIEL)* Tell her she looks good.

DANIEL: You look good.

*(MEG smiles, then thinks better of it.)*

MEG: Next time pick up the phone. You scared everyone. *(Picks up umbrella, starts to head to door.)*

DANIEL: O K.

MEG: I don't care if you skip my calls. But you could at least answer it when it's your mother. We just wanted to congratulate you.

DANIEL: On what?

MEG: On *The New Yorker*. It's really good.

DANIEL: What the hell are you talking about?

(MEG *roots through her bag and pulls out the magazine, opens it to a page marked with a Post-It.*)

MEG: I brought you an extra copy. I'm sure you bought out the Barnes and Noble, but hey, I figured when this kind of thing happens you can never have too many.

DANIEL: (*Slowly, as though she were dumb.*) What are you talking about?

MEG: Your cartoon. (*Hands it to him. Points and smiles.*) It's good. Could've had better placement, but it's good. Your Mom said she literally screamed when she read your name in the corner.

DANIEL: (*Holding and staring at the cartoon.*) I didn't draw this.

(*Blackout*)


### Scene 3

(*Later. Hard rain.* DANIEL *is poring over a cartoon. He sketches with a pencil, unhappy with what he is doing. He stops and starts, unsure of whether or not to even continue. Several times he flips the pencil over and erases, brushing the eraser shreds into* MAN's *lap. After this happens the third time,* MAN *glares at* DANIEL.)

DANIEL: (*Glancing up at him*) Sorry.

(MAN *lifts paper again.* DANIEL *readjusts and sweeps eraser shreds off the other side of the table. Resumes sketching. After a few moments, stops, and erases again. Resumes sketching.* MAN *stands up, folds his paper in half, and sets it down on the table. He walks around behind* DANIEL *and stands with arms akimbo, observing. After a moment*)

DANIEL: Does this look like a building or a rooster? Honestly.

MAN: It looks like...like a penguin...on top of a butter churn.

DANIEL: Is that closer? *(Considers)* I guess that's closer.

MAN: *(Reaching over him, taking the pencil)* Your problem is the context.

DANIEL: What do you \ [mean?]

MAN: *(Pointing with the pencil)* The background. It looks like a farm. Here. There. All of that. There's no grass in a city. Or sunflowers. What are you doing? The flower is half as tall as the building. And how can you not draw a building? That's about the easiest thing in the worl—it's a *rectangle!*

DANIEL: *(Closes the notebook)* O K! That's fine. Thanks.

MAN: Sorry. I didn't mean to offend you.

DANIEL: *(Offended)* You didn't. *(Short pause)* Did you at least get the joke?

MAN: Of course I got it. I just don't know if I wanted it.

DANIEL: Thanks.

MAN: Daniel, why don't you stop working on that and move onto something else?

DANIEL: Just leave me alone. I'm going to finish this and then send it in to *The New Yorker*. Oh and don't you send anymore in for me. It's humiliating.

MAN: *(Laughing)* I didn't. And you're not sending that in.

DANIEL: Yes I am.

MAN: Noooo you're not. You can do a lot better.

DANIEL: Excuse me, but who the hell are you to tell me what I'm capable of?

MAN: You can do better. You know it, too.

DANIEL: This just needs more revision.

MAN: The more you polish shit...

DANIEL: So you think *you* can do a lot better?

MAN: Yeah. I mean, I have. You saw it.

DANIEL: Yeah?

MAN: Yeah.

DANIEL: Fine. Right now. (*Rips a blank page out of the notebook. Hands it to him. Hands him a pencil*) Beat me. Go!

MAN: (*Frantic*) How long?

DANIEL: Go!

(*A race! They each sketch.* DANIEL *constantly looks over. The race goes on a few seconds shorter than could conceivably be required of a cartoon sketch.* DANIEL *makes good use of his eraser. Then...*)

MAN: Done.

DANIEL: What? How can you be done?

MAN: A good idea writes itself.

DANIEL: Show me.

(MAN *slides* DANIEL *the comic.* DANIEL *stares at it a minute. He is genuinely crushed. It is much better than his.*)

DANIEL: This is really good. I mean it's not the kind of thing I go for, but it's...good.

MAN: Thank you. (*Short pause*) What did you draw?

DANIEL: Nevermind.

MAN: Let me see \ [it.]

(DANIEL *crumples his up.*)

MAN: That's just juvenile.

DANIEL: Whatever. I don't care anyway.

(MAN *smiles like a wise parent. Short pause*)

DANIEL: So you're new.

MAN: Yeah.

DANIEL: *(A jocular accusation)* Did you give me a big present?

MAN: You mean the \

DANIEL: About a \ [hundred-and]

MAN: —a-hundred-and-fifty-thousand dollars?

DANIEL: Approximately.

MAN: Did I give that to you?

*(Short pause)*

DANIEL: You gave it to me.

MAN: Daniel.

DANIEL: What?

(MAN *sighs.*)

DANIEL: Don't think I don't appreciate it. I was having some serious financial problems.

MAN: It's a fucked up world.

DANIEL: I know! Wow. I've never heard anyone put it like that before.

MAN: Yeah?

DANIEL: A fucked up world.

MAN: You should really call home.

DANIEL: You hungry?

MAN: Yeah. A bit.

DANIEL: *(Takes a pile of money out of his pocket)* Let's order a pizza.

BOTH: Pineapple.

DANIEL: I don't really have any small bills.

*(MAN takes out his wallet. Looks inside)*

DANIEL: The smallest I have is a hundred. Do you think the pizza guy would take a hundred?

MAN: *(DANIEL looks at him.)* Lemme see. Maybe I have some small bills here.

DANIEL: That's my wallet.

MAN: Ah! A twenty!

DANIEL: You have my wallet.

MAN: *(Examines his wallet)* Oh. Hmmm. I didn't really....this is yours?

DANIEL: I think so. *(Takes wallet from him)* Yeah, this is definitely mine. My Blockbuster card. Credit cards. My I D... *(Takes out and holds up a twist tie)* Twist Tie. *(Looks at exterior of wallet)* You scuffed it up.

MAN: No I didn't. Not intentionally.

DANIEL: This is in much worse condition. It's all battered, like it went through the wash or something.

MAN: I dunno. Stop being a baby. It's a wallet.

DANIEL: I like my wallet. It took me a long time to pick out.

MAN: Right.

DANIEL: Bi-fold, tri-fold. Brown, black. Velcro. Leather...

MAN: Vinyl.

DANIEL: Yeah.

MAN: Sorry, I didn't know it meant that much to you.

DANIEL: It doesn't...I'm just...

MAN: Fixating.

DANIEL: Huh?

MAN: You're fixating, Daniel. You have some real problems. Why don't you sack up and deal with those.

DANIEL: Why don't you...go write a self-help book or get a talk show or, I don't know, take your *fuckin* life, because I don't remember asking for advice.

MAN: You're acting like a child.

DANIEL: *(Short pause. Tries to think of something clever to respond with. Instead:)* Shut up. *(He tries to think of something else. Comes up with:)* Screw you.

MAN: Really, Daniel? "Shut up. Screw You"? That's the best you can come up with? Good thing you're not a writer. And, hey, if you screwed me it would technically be masturbation.

*(Short pause)*

DANIEL: Nice suit.

MAN: Thanks. It's just our style.

DANIEL: Maybe.

MAN: You like it? Want to try it on?

DANIEL: Maybe.

*(MAN takes off the jacket, gives it to DANIEL. He puts it on. The sleeves are too long.)*

DANIEL: I'm still growing?

MAN: Just your arms.

DANIEL: I've been really worried about that. I feel like they've been getting longer!

MAN: It's true. You'll need some new clothes.

DANIEL: That's fine. I can pay for them.

MAN: Right. Look at that. When is the last time you wore a suit?

DANIEL: Graduation?

MAN: *(Squinting. Trying to recall)* Was it...

DANIEL: No. Not graduation. Under the robe I wore one of Meg's thongs.

MAN: *(A moment. Then remembers. Laughs, embarrassed)* Such an \ [idiot.]

DANIEL: *(Laughs)* She was so freaked out...I was too...But the last time I wore a suit was...oh God... it must have been a rented tuxedo maybe? Does that count? Senior Prom. Oh God. High school.

MAN: Kate \ [Mavec]

DANIEL: Carrie Maveccio.

MAN: Carrie! Right. Carrie! Ms Maveccio. The P E student teacher.

*(Long pause. Grins. They are both remembering something dirty. Finally:)*

MAN: I had sex with her behind the snack bar.

DANIEL: I made out with her behind the snack bar.

MAN: No. It was sex. We went all the way.

DANIEL: No, I made out with her but *told* people we went all the way.

MAN: *(Can't quite remember)* I thought...

DANIEL: That's what I always tell my friends when that night comes up. That we did it.

MAN: Are you sure?

*(DANIEL nods.)*

MAN: Really? Hmm... It's funny. You tell yourself something again and again and it eventually becomes the truth.

DANIEL: What?

MAN: When is the moment? That moment of transition. When is the exact instant that you forget something? It has to be an instant. Where if someone were to ask me the actual way it happened, from one second to the next, I would give different answers, or I wouldn't know, or I'd *think* I knew and swear on a stack of bibles that that was how it happened. I can remember sleeping with her. I remember it. But it never happened.

*(Short pause)*

DANIEL: *(Taking off coat. Gives it to MAN)* Do you want this back?

MAN: Why haven't you been sleeping? And why are you chewing that gum?

DANIEL: Why are you even here?

MAN: *(Looks at watch)* I thought I'd kill some time and read the paper here if you don't \ [mind.]

DANIEL: No—please. Be my guest. It's fine. I have some work to do anyway.

*(Short pause. They both return to their tasks—DANIEL to drawing, and MAN to reading the paper.)*

DANIEL: It's rare finding someone like you.

*(A few moments. MAN looks up to DANIEL.)*

MAN: I didn't sleep with her?

*(DANIEL shakes his head.)*

MAN: Damn. I should have.

DANIEL: You're telling me.

*(Blackout)*

## Scene 4

*(The next evening. Light rain. MAN and DANIEL are on opposite sides of the table arm wrestling. They are exerting much effort, but their clasped hands are at equilibrium. DANIEL still chews the gum. MAN is now more disheveled.)*

DANIEL: *(Through clenched teeth. Spoken slowly)* That is nuts.

MAN: *(Also through clenched teeth, slowly)* What is?

DANIEL: I haven't gotten any stronger?

MAN: Well you haven't gotten any weaker. That's something.

DANIEL: Give up, old man.

MAN: You asked me to do this. I said no. You insisted. So now I've gotta win.

DANIEL: I wanted to try it.

MAN: Why?

DANIEL: I don't know. *(Short pause)* I thought maybe... I thought it would be easier to... *(Short pause)* Ive been trying to remember the alarm code to the garage door. *(Short pause)* Am I dying?

*(MAN drops his side. DANIEL wins.)*

DANIEL: Hah!

MAN: It's a waste of time.

DANIEL: Whatever. I won. It was fun.

MAN: So I won.

DANIEL: No, "I now" won.

MAN: And I'm here now and I'm you, so I won.

DANIEL: No, you're me. And I'm— Whatever. I won. It was fun.

MAN: Yeah. Fun.

DANIEL: Hey, lemme ask you something. When you looked at me, the first time, did you get a first impression?

MAN: Huh?

DANIEL: I mean that people have distinct first impressions of people the first time they meet them. But you can never, like, objectively evaluate yourself. So when you looked at me, did you have a first impression? Like in the split second before you realized I'm you, and I'm just "some guy".

MAN: Hmmm. I'm not sure. I thought I looked a little better than I thought I did.

DANIEL: Well that's something.

MAN: Yeah, don't worry...I thought you were *real* cute, Daniel. (*Brief laughter*)

DANIEL: So, shouldn't I be, like, asking you for lottery numbers or something?

MAN: It would just be you guessing them.

DANIEL: Yeah. I guess so.

MAN: I will tell you something, though. I started re-learning Russian.

DANIEL: I was thinking of taking it up again!

MAN: Too bad you never went to the damn class. Could have saved me \ [a ton]

DANIEL: It was at eight A M!

MAN: Was it?

DANIEL: Fine. It was at eleven, but that is still too early to be awake. I don't trust anyone awake before ten. They must be aliens.

MAN: *Dobriy dyenh.* Good day.

DANIEL: Wow. That's right! I remember!

MAN: *Menya zovut Daniil.* My name is Daniel.

DANIEL: *(Deep voiced, like a dictator) Menya zovut Daniil.*

MAN: That's right. Good.

DANIEL: *Dom moego dvayuradnogo brata ochen zateiliv.*

MAN: The house of my cousin is fanciful?

DANIEL: It's what I remember! *(Laughter)* This is great. I'm impressed. I never was good with romance languages.

MAN: Russian is *not* a romance language.

DANIEL: It's not?

MAN: *Ya tebya lublyu.* That's "I love you". Does that sound romantic to you?

DANIEL: Darling, be mine forever because I...because I...How should I put it? *(Again, like a dictator. Slamming fist) Ya tebya lublyu! (Laughter. It subsides.)* Why did you give me a-hundred-and-fifty-thousand-dollars?

MAN: Why did you draw that *New Yorker* cartoon?

DANIEL: Why did I - I didn't. You drew it!

MAN: And I'm you so you drew it.

DANIEL: Stop it. I'm being really annoying right now.

MAN: You drew the cartoon. It is unmistakably filled with your promise. *(Retrieves the magazine which is folded open to the page.)* You like this, right?

DANIEL: Yeah.

MAN: How much?

DANIEL: What are you even \ [doing?]

MAN: Don't fixate on dumb questions. Answer mine. How much do you like this?

*(Short pause)*

DANIEL: I love it. I want it to be mine.

MAN: But it is yours.

DANIEL: I know.

MAN: So why can't you accept it?

DANIEL: I don't \ [know.]

MAN: Yes you do. Because it represents a huge step forward. And that makes you feel uncomfortable. It means you're growing up a little. Don't be embarrassed of it—you're getting better! That's a good thing. Cheer up!

DANIEL: It's not my kind of humor.

MAN: What is your kind of humor?

DANIEL: I can't describe it—YOU KNOW! Why do I even have to explain myself to myself!

MAN: I'm just trying to give you a leg up. How many times do you hear, "Man, I wish I had known that back when I was..." *(Short pause)* Look, I'm just trying to be helpful.

DANIEL: I appreciate it, O K? I appreciate it.

MAN: So why are you creating all of this, Daniel? Someone *stole* your identity?

DANIEL: Someone stole my identity!

MAN: No...

*(MAN puts DANIEL in a headlock.)*

DANIEL: Get off me! Identity theft is very serious! They can really wreck your credit and \ [empty out...]

MAN: Someone stole your identity and is making your life much better. But that didn't happen, did it?

DANIEL: I don't \ [know!]

MAN: Daniel, why can't you say where the money came from?

DANIEL: *(Losing his temper)* YOU gave it to me!

MAN: Is it because by admitting the money's source, you're admitting something else?

DANIEL: I swear to God I have no idea what you are talking about.

*(Short pause.* MAN *releases* DANIEL.*)*

MAN: O K. I don't want to push...

DANIEL: Heh! Right...

MAN: Right. *(Short pause)* If you could have anything in the world, what would it be?

DANIEL: Easy. To have Meg back.

MAN: Is that really what you want?

DANIEL: Sometimes you can be really annoying!

MAN: Ah, you finally notice what everyone else has.

DANIEL: Ha, yeah. Well... She's dating some thirty-five year old physical therapist. I mean, what the hell is that? I bet he interrupts her in the middle of sex and says, "Now, be careful when you bend that way, Meghan! If you're not careful, you're likely to mis-align your vertebrae. Thrust with your legs..."

MAN: You think a lot about them having sex?

DANIEL: No...I dunno. I was just making a joke.

MAN: Do you really want Meg back?

DANIEL: What? Does my fucking hearing deteriorate also? Maybe I should plan ahead and buy a hearing aid now to beat inflation. Yes, you heard what I said. I want Meg back.

MAN: Sorry. *(Short pause)* Why?

DANIEL: Because...because we're perfect together. *(Short pause)* She knows everything about me. And I know everything about her.

MAN: So it's easy?

DANIEL: Is that so bad? It's effortless. How 'bout that. Being with Meg is so good it's effortless.

MAN: So why aren't you with her now?

*(Long pause)*

DANIEL: Because I make her miserable. *(Long pause)* I can't remember the alarm code to the garage door.

MAN: You don't have a garage.

DANIEL: To my garage door at the old house.

MAN: When we were...

DANIEL: Say "you" please. You're freaking me out with all the double shit.

MAN: The garage door to the house on Glenbrooke?

DANIEL: Yeah.

MAN: Four, four, six...

DANIEL: Oh—

MAN: Four, four, six, oh... *(Short pause. Smiles)* I don't remember.

DANIEL: Neither do I. I don't like forgetting.

MAN: Can I say one thing?

DANIEL: What?

MAN: Forgetting isn't so bad. I mean, for every memory that goes out, a new one comes in. Not literally, of course, but I think you know what I'm saying. We meet new people and we learn new alarm codes and some of us... *(Waves* New Yorker*)* ...some of us even draw new things. Good things. It ain't all that bad, I don't think. Forgetting just means we're moving on. Can't fight it.

DANIEL: I've been thinking about that recently.

MAN: I know you have.

DANIEL: I make Meg miserable.

MAN: If you hold onto the past, clasping and clutching it close to your chest, unwilling to let go, then you won't go anywhere.

DANIEL: We're just left with a-hundred-and-fifty thousand pounds in our arms, stuck in the mud. *(Short pause)* Every now and then we have to remind ourselves. We have to remember to forget.

*(Blackout)*

### Scene 5

*(A little later. No rain. It is night time.* MAN *and* DANIEL*)*

MAN: Remind me.

DANIEL: Why would you want that?

MAN: Tell me a story that I've all but forgotten.

DANIEL: Which story?

*(They exchange a glance.)*

DANIEL: I don't \ [know what you're]

MAN: It's O K. You've never told it to anyone before. You still won't be.

DANIEL: This is so fucking dumb, I don't want to \
[do this.]

MAN: *(Immediately)* I am nine years old. My mother and
I are sitting on the carpet \ [of the living room.]

DANIEL: O K stop. Stop. You don't know that you were
nine. I don't know how old I was. You're just starting
the story with "I was nine".

MAN: I guess I was just about that age.

DANIEL: So say that.

MAN: You say it.

*(Short pause)*

DANIEL: I was younger. I don't know how young. Eight,
nine, ten. Whatever. My Mom and I were sitting on the
carpet.

MAN: It's a memory. Don't shave this down.

DANIEL: It's weird to hear it out loud.... My Mom and I
*are* sitting on the carpet. I'm showing her...I'm showing
her a drawing I did at camp.

MAN: What is the drawing?

DANIEL: It's of a prison.

MAN: *(Smiles)* Why would you draw a prison?

DANIEL: *(Defensive)* Because that was the assignment,
O K? We were talking about jails I guess. I dunno. It
was a long time ago.

MAN: Sorry. I didn't mean to... Sorry. What did it look
like?

DANIEL: It looks like a grey cement wall. And there's a
man inside.

MAN: And what else?

DANIEL: There's a window up on the wall. A big open window. No bars. And it's revealing a bright blue sky. The bluest sky you've ever seen. It's freedom, through the window.

MAN: So why isn't the man climbing through and escaping?

DANIEL: Because the window is too high.

MAN: How high?

DANIEL: You are fucking annoying, do you know that?

(MAN *smiles.)*

DANIEL: I hate being psychoanalyzed by myself.

MAN: It's called, "Thinking".

DANIEL: *(Scoffs)* H'yeah. Right. So, you want to know how high that window is? It's *just* high enough that the man can't reach it. Even by jumping. And he has no bed and he has no chair or bucket. Nothing. Just a cement floor. A cement wall. And a big open window, just out of reach.

MAN: It's torturous.

DANIEL: Yeah.

MAN: Elegantly so. Why did you draw that?

DANIEL: The counselor said to draw a prison without bars. We were supposed to think of a reason why someone couldn't escape other than the bars. To see if we could.

MAN: And some people drew a guy surrounded by alligators.

DANIEL: *(Laughs)* Most people did.

MAN: And some people drew an island.

DANIEL: One person drew an island. Melissa drew an island. It got second place.

MAN: They gave awards?

(DANIEL *nods*.)

MAN: But you...

DANIEL: I drew a wide open window. Just out of reach.

MAN: And you won first prize. Best in the whole camp.

DANIEL: Of the people who did art that day. I get a paper plate certificate—with a big number one on it. I got first place.

MAN: How did that make you feel?

DANIEL: It makes me feel proud. The counselor photocopies my drawing and tacks it to the wall.

MAN: Why are you reminding me of this story?

(*Short pause*)

DANIEL: Dad comes home from work. He drops that stupid leather bag on the wood floor. BANG. Every day. BANG. And I hop up from the carpet and I run to him and I show him my picture. "Dad, look at this. I drew it. It's a prison!"

(MAN *laughs*, DANIEL *does not*.)

DANIEL: "It's a prison. I won first place. Do you get it?" And he takes it out of my hand and stares at it for a long time. He's really looking carefully. And he doesn't get it. Then I tell him that I want to be an artist.

MAN: And what did he say?

DANIEL: "You better work a whole lot harder if that's what you wanna be."

MAN: And then what?

DANIEL: And then he goes into the kitchen and makes a salami sandwich. On my paper plate.

*(They laugh.)*

MAN: And this is long before he makes you buy your own art supplies?

DANIEL: You know that.

MAN: And long before he calls your comic strip in the high school paper "confusing", even though you knew there was no way for him to understand it when he didn't even *read* the first three.

DANIEL: You know that too.

MAN: And before he keeps filling your room with the applications to engineering programs. And making a point of calling your work to other people \ [a]

DANIEL: A hobby.

MAN: He didn't like it.

DANIEL: He was just disappointed. And then...then sophomore year when Meg called him an asshole...

MAN: What happened? What did you say to her?

DANIEL: "Shut up. Talk about things you know something about." ...I still feel terrible.

MAN: It was a paper plate, Daniel. It was a picture of a window rendered in colored pencil. And it was a careless thing for him to do.

DANIEL: I thought you said you forgot this story?

MAN: I did.

*(Blackout)*

## Scene 6

*(Some time later.* DANIEL *sits on one side of the table.* MEG *stands on the other, holding a spiral bound stack of papers.* DANIEL *now wears pants and is eating from a tub of hummus, using a quarter as a spoon.* MAN *stands, off to the side, observing.)*

MEG: *(Letting the pages push down the palm of her hand, like it is a scale)* Pretty hefty work here Daniel. Thank you. My futon shall finally be level.

DANIEL: It's different from what you've seen before. Of my stuff that you've seen before, at least.

MEG: I can't wait to read it. Really.

DANIEL: I don't know if it's any good \ [or]

MEG: I'm sure it's good.

DANIEL: I don't care. Well, I mean I care. I hope it's good. I mean, it's a damn kid's book, so who cares, but I dunno. I had the idea so whatever. I just want you to like it.

MEG: I'm sure I will.

DANIEL: I don't want it to be because I wrote it. I really want you to like it because you like it.

MEG: Well...I'll let ya know.

*(Short pause. He is deciding whether or not to ruin the surprise. Gives in)*

DANIEL: Open it. To the first page—the dedication.

*(She does so. She reads while smiling. Then lets out one loud guffaw)*

MEG: I remember that!

DANIEL: I promised.

MEG: *(Smiling, looks down at book)* And you remembered.

MAN: I did. How could I forget?

MEG: *(Looks up to MAN)* So what's next?

MAN: Send it to my Aunt.

MEG: The one who works at—

MAN: *(Crosses. Picks up hummus)* Yeah. Maybe some other publishers directly. Cross my fingers. Offer sexual favors.

MEG: To your Aunt? Good luck with that. Unless it's your Aunt Betty.

MAN: No, I meant...

*(They smile a moment. MAN takes a bite.)*

MEG: Are you eating that with a quarter?

MAN: *(With mouth full.)* Maybe.

MEG: That's gross. Don't you have any chips or pita or anything?

MAN: I have chips.

MEG: Why aren't you using them?

MAN: The quarter was closer.

MEG: You know what else was closer? Your finger. Money is dirty!

*(This hadn't occurred to MAN. He switches to his finger.)*

MEG: When are you going to grow up?

MAN: At least I slept eight hours. And no more gum. That's progress.

MEG: Looks like it. Sweet dreams?

MAN: Actually, yes.

MEG: Oh yeah? What was it?

MAN: You really want to know? (*Puts hummus aside. Wipes hand on pants*)

MEG: Sure.

MAN: You don't want to \ [hear what I...]

MEG: Daniel.

(*Pause*)

MAN: I dreamt I was in a big open room with a window, high up. And I wanted to leave. But there was no door. And it was cold and I just kept repeating, "I need to get out of here, I need to get out." But nothing happened. And I said it again. "I need to get out of here. I need to get out." And still nothing happened. So I sat on the ground and just waited. And I waited and I waited. And it was so cold. And days passed. And months. And years. Waiting and waiting. And I'd given up on asking. I'd given up on hope, really. I'm just sitting there in the cold. Waiting... And then suddenly, and without any real reason, I look up at the window, and there's this arm. Reaching through. And I stand up. And I stretch. And I reach for it. And it reaches for me. And it takes my hand. And it pulls me up. And I am free.

MEG: Did you drink before you went to bed?

MAN: Possibly.

MEG: That's a weird dream.

MAN: (*Laughs*) Yeah. I know...

(*Awkward silence*)

MEG: Oh! I wanted to tell you—you won't believe this. They *finally* reinstalled the mailbox on Midland Ave. Isn't that ridiculous? Took them, what, like \ [four years]

MAN: Meg, my Dad died.

*(Short pause)*

MEG: Oh my God. *(Rushes over to him)* Oh my God. I'm so sorry. *(Embraces)* When did this happen?

MAN: Two months ago.

*(MEG lets go. Moves back)*

MEG: He \

MAN: He died two months ago.

MEG: I don't... Why didn't you tell me?!

MAN: I should have.

MEG: Yes, yes you should have. How could you have \ *(Stops herself)* Are you O K?

MAN: I think I am. Yeah.

MEG: I am so, so sorry, Daniel. It was the \ [?]

MAN: Yeah. It's fine. *(Short pause)* He left me a hundred-and-fifty-thousand dollars... So that's pretty decent of him.

*(Short pause. MEG embraces MAN again. After a moment)*

MAN: My mother was asking if you were there. *(Release)* At the funeral. She likes you.

MEG: I wish I had known. *(Short pause)* Is that why youre wearing a suit?

MAN: Im gonna go visit him.

MEG: First time in ain a

MAN: Couple years.

MEG: Do you want me to go with you?

*(MAN shakes his head "no".)*

MAN: It made me realizeI need you to know that I *(Short pause)* I need to say. *(Short pause)* Ya tebya lublyu Nyet.

MEG:I dont speak Russian.

MAN: *(Laughs)* Its alright

MEG: And neither do you!

MAN: I know...I just needed to say it. *(Short pause)* How *is* the good doctor?

MEG: *(Smiling)* How is the good \ [doctor?]

MAN: How is...the good doctor?

MEG: You want to know? *(Short pause)* Boring as fuck.

*(They laugh. He pulls out his wallet.)*

MEG: Oh, hey, you found it!

MAN: Yes I did.

MEG: Where was it?

MAN: *(Ashamed)* In the dryer.

MEG: So you didn't leave it at Baskin-Robbins? You had that poor manager searching through the dumpster! *(Laughs)* Classic.

MAN: Come on, I offered to do it myself! But he was so helpful. I think he has a crush on me. He always gives me an extra scoop.

MEG: You are a disaster.

MAN: I am not!

MEG: Yeah, good point. I can't think of any other time you screwed up. Oh wait. That's right. You hit a school bus. A big, bright yellow school bus. Probably intentionally. *(Short pause)*

MAN: O K I'm a disaster.

*(They laugh. It peters out. The awkward silence returns.)*

MAN: So...

MEG: So...

MAN: I found out that ducks also have them.

MEG: Have what?

MAN: You know. *(Gestures to his crotch)* They have...

*(*MEG *doesn't remember* MAN's *reference.)*

MAN: Yeah... *(Opens wallet, removes twist tie)* Oh right!
So I found this in here. I remember telling myself not
to throw it away, but I can't for the life of me remember
why.

MEG: Daniel.

MAN: What?

MEG: Daniel.

MAN: What?

MEG: Really?

MAN: What?

*(*DANIEL *rises from the chair, approaches them, takes the
twist tie. She extends her right hand. He twists it around her
ring finger. Then, kisses her briefly on the lips. A moment.
He slowly returns to his seat.)*

MEG: *(To* MAN. *Holds up banded hand)* On my right
hand. Still...

MAN: Oh yes. Can't teach an old dog \

MEG: Yeah, yeah, yeah.

*(*DANIEL *lifts comics. Reads)*

MAN: I suppose you gotta go.

MEG: I should. *(Starts to exit. Stops)* Daniel. I'm really
glad you called. I've been thinking about your offer.

MAN: What offer?

MEG: Dinner. You know. When you offered...I was
thinking, you know, we should grab a meal. We haven't

talked in a while, well, really talked, and since I don't have dinner plans I thought we might as well \ [grab]

MAN: I'm busy.

MEG: Oh. Well. Oh. Maybe another \ [time.]

MAN: I'm gonna be busy.

*(Short pause)*

MEG: Right. Of course. *(Embarrassed. Almost exits)*

MAN: But if we did. If we did have dinner, I mean. I would have bought you a-hundred-fifty-thousand-dollar salad.

MEG: Save your pennies, Rich Boy.

MAN: Rich Man.

MEG: *(Singing a bit from* If I Were a Rich Man*)* Ya-ba-dibb-a-dibb-a-dibb-a-deeba-deeba-deeba-deeba-dum.

MAN: Huh?

MEG: It's from... Ya know? Don't worry about it. You sure you don't want some company?

MAN: It's O K. I'm gonna be O K.

MEG: I know you are. *(Exits)*

*(*MAN *looks to* DANIEL.*)*

*(Pause)*

MAN: We're gonna be O K.

*(Blackout)*

END OF PLAY